Business Analysis Book of Mentors

25 Lessons Learned from Seasoned BA Professionals

Compiled by David Barrett and Sandee Vincent

First Edition

StringBean Publishing

Toronto, Ontario

Business Analysis Book of Mentors

25 Lessons Learned from Seasoned Business BA Professionals

Compiled by David Barrett and Sandee Vincent

Published by: StringBean Publishing

Production © 2015 by StringBean Publishing Inc.
Text © 2015 by the authors of each chapter.

Paperback SBN-13: 9781506184555

Published in Canada.

Table of Contents

Asking Questions 3

    Being a Great BA Means… 5

    Asking Yourself, "Does This Make Sense?" 13

    How Do I Know What Questions to Ask? 21

Stakeholders and Change 33

    Know Your Stakeholders 35

    Walk in Their Shoes 43

    Multicultural Challenges 47

    Working With Head, Heart, and Hand 59

    Creating Effective One-Page Documents to Establish Shared Understanding 69

    The Business Therapist 77

Technology 85

    In Defense of Systems Analysis 87

    Achieving Clarity of Thought 93

Seeing the Big Picture 103

    Solve the Right Problem by Understanding the Big Picture 105

    Focus on What Makes Your Business Smart: Business Rules 117

    Design Thinking: Taking Business Analysis to the Next Level 129

To Innovate, to Thrive, to Plan 137

    It's All in the Plan 139

    BA 3.0: Thriving in the Marketplace 149

    A Business Analyst Is a Key Agent of Innovation 159

Communication and Leadership 169

Will the Real Business Analysts (BAs) Please Stand Up—Building a Capable Business Analysis Team 171

What, Not *Who* or *How*—Getting to the Essence 191

Leadership in Business Analysis 205

Just Assumptions, Sound the Alarm! 213

Six Improvisation Lessons for Better Business Analysis 223

Pssst … Can you keep a secret? 231

Find Your Gaps 239

Passion **245**

Love What You Do, or Don't Do it! 247

Closing **257**

List of Authors

Amuchastegui, Maria 87
Barret, Kathleen 105
Barrett, David 239
Barris, John 93
Beaulieu, Christine 47
Crawford, Mike 77
Davis, Barbara 205
Giles, Kevin 13
Gorai, Jared 139
Hass, Kitty 171
Kupersmith, Kupe 223
Lam, Gladys 117
MacPherson, Rod 43
Miller, Roxanne 21
Mohamed, Yamo 247
Mutunga, Paskwa 159
Nituch, Jonathan 35
Payette, Jay 129
Podewsa, Howard 5
Rawsthorne, David 59
Sharp, Alex 191
Thaker, Sohail 149
Thomas, Haydn 213
Van Abbema Patrick 69
Vincent, Sandee 231

Dedication

I am dedicating this book to the 17 people who attended the dinner event held at the Royal York Hotel in Toronto on June 25, 2003 when we coined the idea of an association for business analysts.
– David Barrett

For my father who always had patience to answer my continuous barrage of questions, thus encouraging a passion to understand the what's and why's of life, which continues still.
– Sandee Vincent

Introduction

Business Analysts (BAs) are expected to hit the job running, and not only as systems analysts but increasingly in business advisory and management consultancy roles. Yet, how? You might be new to the job, company, technology, or all of the above. Often, there is no one to ask for guidance, and with business analysis still maturing, not much is written about the subject. How can you quickly gain years upon years of experience in two hours? Thus, the inspiration for this book, *The Business Analysis Book of Mentors: 25 Lessons Learned by Seasoned BA Professionals*. Through the telling of our key lessons gained through experience in leading business analyst roles, you now have 25 mentors at your disposal.

This book is not one you read once and put away, but a resource you will refer to often in your role as a business analyst. BAs work with that one uncontrollable and uncountable variable, people—an increasingly important dimension as BAs are asked to fulfill overlapping roles as project managers and consultants. As much as you can plan and apply a methodology, the unknown quantity, people, is inevitably where most BAs could use a mentor's advice. Consider a conversation Bob had with John one day.

"Bob, have you a minute?" asked John, hovering at the door of

Bob's office.

"Sure, what's up, John?" Bob said curiously. "Come on in, have a seat." John didn't often drop by Bob's office. In fact, John rarely left his desk tucked far back against the windows. John could be counted on to have the most recent figures on just about anything, from baseball stats to the next quarter's sales projections. His new assignment, though, John found more intimidating than an encounter with auditors.

"It's about this project I'm working on. I've never worked with semiconductor technology or users from the field. I just don't know where to start. I'm hoping you can advise me on how to start analyzing a new technology and perhaps give me a few pointers on how to work with the field engineers."

Does this sound familiar? Can you remember being a new BA or the *only* BA in your company, and you wished you had had a Bob on which you could drop in? Here are 25 Bobs, or seasoned BAs, to share their one best piece of advice for success in business analysis. The result of their collective experience is this book.

> *"The mediocre teacher tells. The good teacher explains. The superior teacher demonstrates. The great teacher inspires."*
> —William Arthur Ward

These are our stories, written with humor, jest, sincerity, and analogies, but always with the hope of providing inspiration. Our wish by telling our stories is to not only tell, explain, and demonstrate, but also to inspire you—in your role as a business analyst, and a mentor to other BAs to come. We look forward to adding your key lessons to future editions.

- David and Sandee

Asking Questions

"You can tell whether a man is clever by his answers. You can tell whether a man is wise by his questions." - Naguib Mahfouz (Nobel Prize Winner)

1
Being a Great BA Means…

Howard Podeswa

Being a great BA means asking everything you—and everyone else—wants to know but are afraid to ask.

Would you pretend you know how to do be a brain surgeon? Probably not, but many BAs leave meetings pretending to know everything that was said, when in reality they were too afraid to ask questions if they thought everyone else understood the concept or proposal. If you suffer from the same sort of fear, you have to get over your shyness because leaving those questions unasked will affect the quality of your analysis, and current and future performance—yours and your client's.

I received my first life lesson in engaging in such avoidant behavior in my first business analysis assignment. I started out in IT as a coder working for Atomic Energy of Canada on a simulation program. The work—a combination of chemical/nuclear engineering and programming—kept me in my comfort zone and far from business, an area in which I had no knowledge or interest. So, it was a shock when I moved from there to a small start-up that had much in common with today's agile environments—run by self-organizing teams in which I could be programming, testing, gathering requirements, installing or training end users, all on the same project, depending on what was needed.

On my first assignment, I was asked to visit a client site to evaluate changes to a GL/AP/AR package so I could implement them in the code. I was just days into my new job, and I didn't even know what "GL," "AR," or "AP" stood for, yet there I was heading out to gather requirements for business systems of which I knew nothing about.

Since you will inevitably have to face this situation as a BA, you need to be able to find a way to overcome your embarrassment and ask those *dumb questions*. If you fake it and pretend to understand what you don't, you'll assume wrongly and be ineffective at your main raison d'être as a BA—to be an assimilator and communicator. I wish I could say you need to face this only at the beginning of your career, but the bad news is it never stops happening—at least not to me.

The BA as the Double Outsider

Recently in a phone call, I finally screwed up the courage to ask stakeholders for the full name of a group everyone had been referring to only by its acronym. Embarrassed, I learned that it stood for one of their main business groups, but they explained it, and *we moved on*. The confidence that comes from knowing what clients "pay me the big bucks" for—and what they seek in any good BA—made it easier for me to ask. And I can tell you that it is *not* insider knowledge clients seek from the BA; they already have it. It's the reverse—an outsider's perspective. The BA is a *double outsider*—who is neither *of the business* nor *of the technology* group. I've learned to embrace this outsider status as a core value-added service of a BA who makes it almost gutsy to ask the *stupid* questions from which everyone else shies away.

So, back to that day in the GL world. What did I do? It suddenly occurred to me that I could get the client to teach me the business without (fully) exposing my ignorance. I asked him to pretend I knew nothing about the business process. If he mentioned a term I didn't know—not just the *big words*, but also ones I would have been expected to know (such as *debit* and *credit*)—I'd ask him to "Explain it to me"—you know, "just so I can tell the programmers." (What I didn't mention was that *I* was the chief programmer.)

I'm still using a variation of the same technique, but I've taken it to another level—the CEO level. These days, I'm more likely to say something like, "Assume I know nothing ... so I can explain it to the CEO." (or the CIO, VP, or Steering Committee). I need to keep reminding myself that the people in front of me have called me in, not because I am an industry or technology expert, but because I am a third eye who can look at what they propose without assumptions. I am expected to give them an objective opinion about whether an idea makes sense from a business perspective, ensure business interests are protected as the initiative moves forward, and flag and mitigate risks of future problems with solution providers. In short, they want me because I am not one of them, and as an outsider, I ask the *obvious* questions no one else does.

Those obvious questions fall under one of the following types. They are the questions you will often be the only one in the room asking, but clients seek your ability to get straight answers to them, even if you have to risk looking like a fool to deliver.

Questions about Business Terminology

BAs who've recently migrated from IT often find themselves confronted with business jargon they don't understand, as do independent BA consultants who, like me, hop around frequently from business area to business area. I head off any potential embarrassment before it happens by setting expectations upfront about where my expertise lies (and where it does not); this makes it easier to ask questions about the business terminology and concepts when they come up. (Remember, I don't claim to be an expert in the business area, but an excellent communicator and analyst.)

Besides the business acronyms and jargon everyone else in the room but me seems to understand, I've also run into terms that everyone *thinks* they understand, but don't—at least not all in the same way. For example, I was once with a group of stakeholders discussing requirements of "Product Groups" for a foreign telecom company. The group had bandied a term about for a while, but no one had defined it, so I finally asked, "What exactly do *you* mean when you use that term? Quite probably others will misinterpret it." It turned out half the stakeholders were talking about a package of telecom services marketed and priced together, whereas the others were talking about the particular set of services attached to an individual telephone line. It helped that I could pull out some BA techniques (such as business domain modeling) to structure the conversation, but if I hadn't had the courage to ask, I would have walked out of the meeting with requirements that half the group thought were for something else.

Questions about the Technology

A good BA should not be intimidated by technical jargon. I always keep in mind that behind the jargon is something which can be simply explained. For example, I recently reviewed requirements for a project initiated by the technical side of a company. I had to get past mountains of specs and jargon during a meeting to ask the simple question, "Are we talking here about a customization project, an out-of-the-box solution, or an architectural layer that is not visible to end users?" Surprisingly, no one present could answer that question easily, which immediately told me that it was a question worth asking.

I learned that the system they wanted to purchase came with both an application layer and a set of underlying data tables, but the tables would be empty. A big part of the estimated cost was the need to populate those tables with data from a variety of sources. This was never clearly explained in any documentation the technology group prepared because everyone on its side already understood it. The business side did not, but because I had asked, I could explain the high estimate for technical services in nontechnical terms business decision makers could comprehend.

Basic Assumptions

Basic assumptions refer to issues everyone assumes have already been addressed, so "Why question them?" Sometimes these assumptions are about the solution, as happened, for example, when I consulted on a project to purchase and integrate a "big data" analytics package. Everyone had already moved beyond first principles to look at the integration requirements for the package. But I focused my questions on what I saw as an unchallenged assumption: What was the problem they were trying to solve, and why did they assume data analytics was the solution?

They explained the objective was to reduce *churn*—the rate of customer loss—and presented me with the vendor literature about the "complex mathematics" used to predict customer behavior. Not easily intimidated by technical jargon (see above), I pushed further by asking if they had thought of using more direct predictive measures—such as running experiments on selected groups of customers—and basing their predictions on observed behavior of real people rather than abstract mathematical algorithms. No one had thought about it—at least, until I asked the question.

The Elephant in the Room

The most difficult questions are those everyone thinks about, but no one wants to raise for *political reasons*, which often translates as fear of bruising someone's ego. My company is often asked to evaluate the quality of requirements documentation and processes to flag the risks of a project. Sometimes we can't find anything wrong with the requirements, but find other aspects puzzling, such as the time that has passed since a project was initiated. An uncomfortable question I am then driven to ask is, "Why has this taken so long?"—and the answers I get can point to deficiencies in how funding priorities are set, projects are staged, or dependencies are managed, which are the real risks to the project as it moves forward.

When I look at trends in business analysis, I see the importance of this advice only growing over time. On the one hand, those without training in business analysis increasingly find themselves performing the function of business analyst (even if they don't have the title) thanks to agile work practices and the preference for multifunctional team members. The most important advice I can give them is not to be intimidated by the experts on the *other side*, but to be secure in the knowledge that they will understand everything they need to know—as long as they are unafraid to ask.

On the other hand, as the formal BA role matures and evolves into one of strategic consultant at the executive level, the temptation is greater than ever to hide your ignorance behind a false impression that you know things you don't. If your fear is getting the better of you, remember this: If things go south because you failed to ask an important question, it's not just embarrassing; it can sink your career. But if everything goes well, everyone will remember you as a hero, and they'll quickly forget that you were (or forgive you for having been) the one asking all those annoying questions along the way.

Howard Podeswa
Noble Inc.
401 Richmond St. West, Suite 355
Toronto, ON
Canada M5V-3A8
T 416-532-2205
E-mail: Howardpodeswa@nobleinc.ca
Website: www.nobleinc.ca
Blog: ModernAnalyst.com
Books:
The Business Analyst's Handbook
UML for the IT Business Analyst

Howard Podeswa is a leader in business analysis, having contributed to the formalization of the profession as SME for CompTIA's NITAS BA apprenticeship program, a member of the BABOK review team, and a respected author and practitioner. He has more than 30 years' experience in many aspects of the IT industry, beginning as a developer for Atomic Energy of Canada, Ltd. and subsequently becoming systems analyst, BA, and CEO of Noble Inc. He is the author of two books that have become staples in many BA libraries: *The Business Analyst's Handbook* and *UML for the IT Business Analyst*, now in its second edition and published in three languages.

Through his company, Noble Inc., Howard has provided BA consulting and training services to a broad range of industry sectors, including healthcare, defense, energy, government, and finance for a diverse client base that includes the Mayo Clinic, ISO, Moody's, the Canadian Air Force, the South African Community Peace Program (CPP), Deloitte, UST Global (US and India), TELUS, and BMO/Harris Bank.

Howard is a widely requested speaker at international BA and IT events, most recently at the Norway Developers Conference (NDC 2013), where he spoke on the agile BA, BA Forum (Warsaw) and BA World Conferences across North America. In addition, Howard has designed BA training programs for many corporate education and academic institutions such as Boston University, Humber College, and New Horizons. In his *spare time*, he also runs a parallel life as a professional artist.

2

Asking Yourself, "Does This Make Sense?"

Kevin Giles

To me, business analysis is the best job in the world. No two days are ever the same; you are constantly exposed to new situations, and you have the opportunity to work with lots of interesting people. Being a business analyst, however, comes with much responsibility. As the saying goes, "With great power … "—well, you get the idea.

One scenario that gets the hairs on the back of my neck to stand up is asking another analyst a *why* question about a requirement or a proposed solution and getting the answer, "Well, I don't really understand what the business is looking for, but this is what they said they wanted, so that is what I wrote down." As an analyst, one of our key roles is to understand the basic needs of the business, even in cases when they are not explicitly stated to us. I've had many sleep-deprived nights contemplating—

- What is the business really looking for?
- What problem are we really trying to solve?
- Have I thought of all relevant business scenarios?
- What are the downstream impacts on implementing solution X over Y?
- Is there a better solution to this problem?
- Have we identified the core business issues?
- Is it better to implement a tactical solution instead of a strategic solution?
- Are we solving the right problem?
- Is this solution feasible?
- And so on.

Does This Make Sense?

All these questions can be boiled down to the simple question, "Does this make sense?"—or more specifically, "Based on everything I know about the current problem, solution options, needs, organizational capabilities, risks, and so on, does the decision we are making make sense?" I have found that if I can answer yes to this question, the likelihood that the business will be satisfied with the outcome at the end of the project increases immensely (and I sleep better at night).

Asking yourself, "Does this make sense?" is almost the same as asking a stakeholder "Why?," but it is more of an internal question. To show you I'm not entirely crazy, here is an example: Once, a senior business user came to me with the following requirement. "I need a report that merges data from our operational data store (ODS) to a Microsoft Access database so we can distribute information packages to select clients annually, or as required when there is a change to an investment product we sell."

This request is not bad from a requirements perspective. It tells me what the business needs and why they need it. But does it make sense? It would have been easy for me to go ahead and write a specifications document for the new report, have a developer implement an ODBC connection to the ODS, and then build the required report in Microsoft Access. However, this solution didn't feel right. Table 1 outlines what happened.

Table 1 – Does This Make Sense Q&A

My asking myself whether this makes sense	What I asked the Senior Business User	Answer I received from the Senior Business User
Does it make sense to connect a Microsoft Access database to our corporate ODS to generate a client report? Nope, this seems like a quick solution to a problem—not a strategic response. I had better figure out why they are trying to do this.	What is this Access database used for, and why do you need to connect it to the ODS?	Well, the Access Database tracks clients that have opted in to receive annual information packages on our investment products. We need to get information from the ODS because it contains the most current client address information and investments.
	Do you know why this Access database was created?	I wasn't involved with its build, as it was created by a vendor we used to distribute the information packages

My asking myself whether this makes sense	What I asked the Senior Business User	Answer I received from the Senior Business User
		to our clients. Now that we will be doing this work ourselves, we need to ensure these packages are distributed to the client. This is a regulatory requirement for us.
Hmm, interesting. Why did they stop having the vendor do this work? Maybe just a report will work. I wonder whether there are any problems with cross-referencing clients between the two systems. I had better ask this question.	Why was the decision made to bring this work in-house? What was wrong with the previous process?	Well, we had many complaints from clients who were not receiving the packages they requested. We had no way to verify which clients should receive packages, as only the vendor had this information. In addition, sometimes the packages were sent to old client addresses because we received the address updates, but these were never provided to the vendor.
This is all quite interesting. Now I	Can you tell me what the basic	Well, the regulations stipulate that if a

My asking myself whether this makes sense	What I asked the Senior Business User	Answer I received from the Senior Business User
need to understand more about the requirements for opting in to receive this information.	requirements are for a client opting in to receive these information packages? Note that in the real world, this was a series of specific and general questions.	client requests (opt-in) it, we must send an annual package containing information on all their investments. A package must also be sent if we significantly change the investment products. We need to meet this requirement, but we don't want to send these packages out to all our clients, as this would be very expensive.
Well, this makes sense now. I now understand the core requirement and reasons the report was requested. But I have another idea …	If we added an "Opt-in Indicator" to our client information system and changed the business process for collecting these opt-in notifications, couldn't you then pull the mailing list you require directly from our ODS?	Yes. Not only could I do that, but we also could use this information for tracking the size of this distribution list over time and begin using it for budget forecasting. You know what, we have three other important distribution

My asking myself whether this makes sense	What I asked the Senior Business User	Answer I received from the Senior Business User
		lists we manage manually. Could we add these?

As you can see from this example, what started as a simple report request evolved into simple operational system enhancements. From a purely selfish perspective, it would have been easier to design the report as requested. However, through the pursuit of understanding, a more appropriate and better solution was implemented without a significant increase in cost—better for both the organization and client group.

Drilling Down to the Core Requirements

The key point to take away from this example? While doing some due diligence and drilling down from the initial request to the basic business requirement, my role changed from an order taker ("build this report for me") to a strategic partner ("let's work together to identify and solve a basic business problem"). I'm not saying it is never right to just "add this field to this screen" or "implement this report" when requested by the business. However, it is always critical for the analyst to understand the underlying needs, reasons, or drivers for doing so.

Not only is this good for the organization but, from a development team perspective, the closer you get to the core needs or requirements of the business, the more creative you can be with the solutions you can develop. For example, I have been looking for a new car. If I told the salesperson my requirement is "I need a BMW 3 Series Sedan," it would be reasonable to expect him or her to try to sell me various new and used BMW 3 Series Sedans. However, this requirement doesn't make much sense. Why a BMW 3 Series Sedan?

Instead, if I said I need a vehicle that 1) gets good gas mileage, 2) has four doors so the kids can get in and out of the back, and 3) is semi-sporty so I can still feel a little cool, the solution still might be a BMW 3 Series Sedan, but many other solution options become available. Think about this scenario. Is it any different from having a requirement that states, "Create the XYZ Report" without providing justification that this is the appropriate solution for the organization? You are doing the development/solution team and business stakeholders a huge favor if you can capture the true requirements and let the solution design be shaped by the requirements and superior technical skills and abilities of the technical experts.

Importantly, you need to ask, "Does this make sense?" repeatedly throughout the life cycle of a project. Even if the answer is yes early in the project, the answer could easily change to no based on changes in priority, newly discovered information, stakeholder changes, solution limitations, and so on. In a busy world, it is often difficult to take the time to slow down, really look at the information given to you, and ask, "Does this make sense?" However, it is critical that you, as an analyst, ask this question. Doing so increases the value you provide to your business stakeholders and solution development teams.

Kevin Giles
Senior Business Analyst
Norima Consulting Inc.
1101- 220 Portage Avenue
Winnipeg, MB
Canada R3C 0A5
T 204-272-7170 M 204-791-9124
E-mail:
kevin.giles@norimaconsulting.com
Twitter: @wpganalyst

Kevin has worked as a business and systems analyst for 12 years in Winnipeg, Manitoba. He has a passion for trying to simplify the complex and takes great pride in reducing the documentation he produces daily. Kevin believes a good model is worth its weight in gold and seeks innovative ways to apply established modeling techniques. He is active in the BA community as past president, VP of Professional Development and VP of Communications for the IIBA Winnipeg Chapter. Kevin loves being a business analyst with all its difficulties and appreciates the opportunities, relationships, and experiences the profession has provided him. Besides being a business analyst, Kevin is also a father to his daughter Katherine and son Nolan, and married to his lovely wife Liz.

3

How Do I Know What Questions to Ask?

Roxanne Miller

The Man Who Asked Questions

"About 2,400 years ago in Athens a man was put to death for asking too many questions," opens a chapter in Nigel Warburton's book *A Little History of Philosophy*. "Snub-nosed, podgy, shabby, and a bit strange, Socrates did not fit in,". Viewed by people as charismatic with a brilliant mind, Socrates was unique, but also very annoying. As Socrates shuffled around the marketplace, he often stopped people and asked them straightforward—yet awkward—questions.

Socrates was (the first)/(an early) requirements manager. The philosopher systematically questioned processes and systems, and the people and thinking behind them. The meaning of *philosopher* in Greek is "love of wisdom." Effective business analysts understand that the value of wisdom is still based on reasoning and asking questions, and not on believing something simply because someone important told you it was true. Wisdom, according to Socrates, isn't about knowing many facts and the way to do something. Rather, wisdom is understanding the nature of our existence and the limits of what we can know.

Despite the endurance of the Greek philosopher's advice, tomes have been written on governments and businesses who have failed to apply critical reasoning.

The Team Who Didn't Ask Enough Questions

About 20 years ago, a team of consultants for a global software company experienced such a tragic end to a project. Thankfully, unlike Socrates, they were not put to death. However, some consultants lost their employment for not asking the right questions. The team should have asked, "What currencies must this banking system process?" The system was developed to process its national currency, but it also needed to process United States dollars. The tragic ending to the project was that the company involved was forced out of business by its national government for noncompliance.

How can you avoid tragic project outcomes? Get better at asking questions!

The Requirements Management Process

To do so, I am going to introduce you to a proven requirements management process. Together, we will:

- Explore a classification of stakeholder roles in a requirements management process
- Identify six requirements focus points

- Understand a structure for asking questions—the requirements framework

I use a simple classification of roles in a requirements management process, as shown in Figure 1, to organize and identify potential stakeholders at the start of a project and throughout the development and implementation phases. Next, I explore six areas of interest (requirements focus points) for asking questions. Finally, I tie the roles and focus points together in what I call the requirements framework.

Through the Eyes of a Requirements Producer

As Socrates expounded on the virtues of teamwork: "Two heads are better than one." The collaborative efforts of all the stakeholders dramatically increase the accuracy of the requirements gathered and significantly reduce the likelihood that requirements are missed. Simply defined, a stakeholder is anyone with whom I collaborate during the requirements management process.

Let's define our stakeholder roles (Figure 1). I am going to describe my approach to asking questions from the viewpoint of a requirements producer. A *requirements producer* is any individual responsible for capturing the requirements (eliciting, analyzing, representing, and coordinating the validation and approval of the requirements). He or she is also responsible for managing the requirements to ensure compliance and integration throughout the development and installation of the system. *Business analysis* is a term commonly used to encompass the activities performed by the requirements producer, and many organizations use *business analyst* as a job title for this role.

The *requirements supplier* is any individual responsible for defining the business needs to be satisfied, which includes supplying all the detail from the initial idea, or inception, through each incremental iteration of the system development and implementation. A *requirements receiver* is any individual who receives and uses the requirements specifications as the input to develop work products for implementing the requirements. Finally, a *requirements supporter* is any individual who is a champion of improving and sustaining the requirements process (ideally, everyone plays this role).

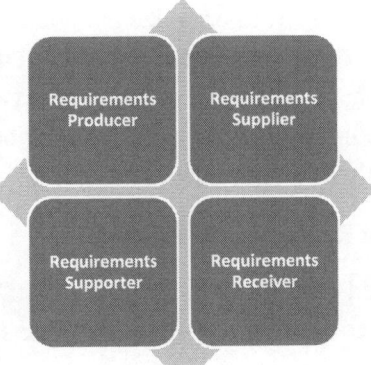

FIGURE 1. Roles in a Requirements Management Process

I consider the requirements suppliers and requirements receivers to be my key contributors, and ask questions of the people in these two roles primarily. The stakeholder profiling technique allows you to identify whom you need to engage and how to plan to engage them. The stakeholder profiling technique is explained in more detail in chapter 2 of my book, *The Quest for Software Requirements* (Miller, 2009).

Requirements Focus Points

From a requirements management perspective, all businesses are the same. In my role as a business analyst consultant, it doesn't matter to me what my client's business is. My approach to asking questions is the same regardless of industry or type of project.

In its essence, every business can be described as the transfer of information and materials from one party to another. I could broaden this description by including *the exchange of goods and services between parties*. However, I want to keep the concept simple. By focusing on this basic business description, I can understand the business as a whole first and then progress to the detailed complexities (usually because of technology). As technologies advance, businesses evolve and apply the technologies with the goal of making *the transfer of information and materials from one party to another* faster and cheaper.

Keeping in mind that all businesses perform the same basic function (*the transfer of information and materials from one party to another),* you can formulate questions in an iterative and incremental cycle. The six logical areas of interest to address are shown in Figure 2.

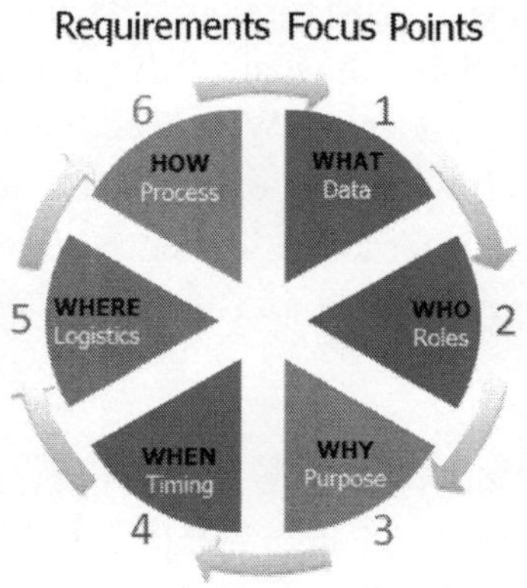

Requirements Focus Points

FIGURE 2. Requirements Focus Points

Although the sequence for asking questions should not matter, I use the following order starting with *What*:

1. What (Data)—What information and materials are needed? The focus here is on data (information and materials). Simply stated, *What* is needed? Ignore the technology for now, and just ask what data are used, stored, calculated, retrieved, and transferred.
2. Who (Roles)—Who needs the information and materials? This area of interest focuses on who or what (in the case of automation). These Who's and What's are called roles. In summary, Who needs the What?
3. Why (Purpose)—Why are the information and materials needed? Defining the why or purpose, establishes a common

understanding of the project. Ask questions to find out Why the Who needs the What. In an interview with someone who represents the role, you might ask, "Why do you want this information?" or "What is the purpose of having this information?" The Why often describes the reason for, or the work performed by, a role.

4. When (Timing)—When are the information and materials needed? When is the information needed or required? Is it needed to trigger, assist, or complete another process?. Incrementally build on what you've already elicited. For each Why and When, does the Who need the What? When is often associated with what time of day in a time zone. However, When can also refer to the sequence of events, triggers, and business cycles; and the transformation of states.

5. Where (Logistics)—Where are the information and materials used? Continuing to incrementally build on the previous interests, for each Who and Why, Where is the What used?

6. How (Process)—How are the information and materials used? This area of interest focuses on procedures and process. Note that this is not to be confused with how to design the system. How does the Who use the What?

"It is better to ask a few well-thought-out questions, than a lot of questions without thinking."

Requirements Framework

The six requirements focus points and the stakeholder viewpoints (suppliers and receivers) are combined to form a structure for asking questions called a *requirements framework,* based on John Zachman's framework (Zachman, 1987). Whereas the *software development lifecycle (SDLC)* defines the stages or phases required to develop a system, a requirements framework defines the perspectives of the roles in the development lifecycle and viewpoint of each role in developing and implementing requirements throughout the lifecycle stages. Although agreeing in general with the meaning behind Zachman's framework, for simplicity, I respectfully modified the matrix to coincide with the application on eliciting requirements. A detailed explanation of the modifications is included in chapter 1 of *The Quest for Software Requirements* (Miller, 2009). The resulting modified version of the requirements framework is shown in Table 2.

Requirements Framework Perspectives (Rows)

The matrix rows represent the different perspectives or viewpoints of the contributing requirements roles:

- Requirements Supplier's View: The requirements supplier is any individual responsible for defining the business needs to be satisfied, which includes supplying all the details from the initial idea, or inception, through each incremental iteration of system development. The requirements supplier's view includes scope, business models, and operations. Scope defines the vision and mission of the enterprise. Business models convey the conceptual nature of the business (structure, processes, organization, and so on). Operations define what the new system will be.

- Requirements Receiver's View: A requirements receiver is any individual who receives and uses the requirements specifications as the input to develop work products for implementing the requirements. They assist in the requirements process by validating individual requirements, primarily for feasibility, completeness, and conflicts. They can assist in validating additional quality characteristics such as necessity, priority, and traceability. The requirements receiver's view includes system, technology, and components aspects of development. System models are used to explore optional solutions. Technology and construction components are used to demonstrate the feasibility of the system under development.

Requirement Framework Areas of Interest (Columns)

The matrix columns represent the areas of interest viewed from each perspective.

- DATA (what): This column relates to the information used by the enterprise. Functional requirements describe the data whereas the nonfunctional requirements are about the data.

- ROLES (who): This column comprises the people and organizations or other systems involved or that interact with the business enterprise. The functional requirements address the interaction between the role and the business process whereas the nonfunctional requirements are about taking care of the roles.

- PURPOSE (why): The motivation behind what the business does is described in this column. The functional requirements describe the ends and means whereas the nonfunctional requirements describe the environment to support the accomplishment of the ends and means.

- TIMING (when): This column identifies the effects of time on the business enterprise. Functional requirements describe the processing of events whereas nonfunctional requirements describe the timing of the events.

- LOGISTICS (where): Logistics concerns the geographical distribution of the data and functions of the enterprise. Functional requirements describe locations whereas nonfunctional requirements support the locations.

- PROCESS (how): This column incorporates the processes and procedures the enterprise executes. Functional requirements describe the processes whereas nonfunctional requirements support the processes.

Table 2. Requirements Framework

	DATA (what)	ROLES (who)	PURPOSE (why)	TIMING (when)	LOGISTICS (where)	PROCESS (how)
Scope, Business Model, Operations Requirements Supplier's View	Identify and define the data used by the business enterprise	Identify and define who performs a role in the business processes	Identify and define the business goals and strategies	Identify and define the events and triggers of business processing	Identify and define the enterprise locations and network	Identify and define processes and procedures of the business
System Model, Design, Construction Requirements Receiver's View	Design, construct, and test data entities	Design, construct, and test interfaces and system work	Design, construct, and test the system to enforce business rules	Design, construct, and test system cycles	Design, construct, and test system location and network	Design, construct, and test system process-ing

Requirements Framework Applied

The requirements framework described above is used as the foundation for organizing the lists of possible elicitation questions contained in Part II of *The Quest for Software Requirements* (Miller, 2009). The book presents more than 2,000 suggested questions across 14 nonfunctional categories. The questions are first grouped under the six areas of interest and further separated by perspective (suppliers and receivers).

Examples of questions that may be asked to elicit reliability requirements (*reliability* is the extent to which the system consistently performs the specified functions without failure) are shown in Table 3.

Table 3. Example Reliability Questions

	Requirements Supplier Perspective	Requirements Receiver Perspective
Data	What system failure reports are needed?	What data exist for use in rigorous testing to achieve the level of desired reliability?
Roles	What users have a greater need for reliability?	Who is called when system outages occur?
Purpose	What is the cost of lost business when the expected level of reliability is not achieved?	What is the history/track record for similar installations of vendor components?
Timing	During what periods are system reliability most critical?	When are system upgrades and fixes migrated into production?
Logistics	How does system reliability vary by business location?	What resources are needed at each business location to restore a system?
Process	What escalation procedures are required during an outage?	How is the system monitored for detection of errors that do not cause an outage?

References

Miller, Roxanne E. *The Quest for Software Requirements*. Milwaukee, MI: MavenMark Books, 2009. PDF version available at http://requirementsquest.com.

Zachman, John A. "A Framework for Information Systems Architecture." *IBM Systems Journal* 26, no. 3 (1987): 276.

Roxanne Miller, Requirements Quest, Inc.
Twitter: @ReqSuperFreak

Website: www.RequirementsQuest.com
LinkedIn: www.linkedin.com/in/RequirementsQuest

 A self-proclaimed "Requirements Super Freak," Roxanne Miller has consulted on requirements process improvement and business analysis best practices for more than 20 years. Roxanne is an active member of the IIBA® and a Certified Business Analysis Professional™ (CBAP®). She founded the IIBA Greater Madison Chapter, Wisconsin, USA, and served as president from 2006 to 2011. Additionally, Roxanne helped Wisconsin IIBA chapters unite and launch an annual event, WI BADD® (Wisconsin Business Analyst Development Day; www.wibadd.org), which is devoted to education, development, and networking opportunities for business analysis professionals.

Roxanne's book, *The Quest for Software Requirements*, is a first-of-its-kind reference guide with more than 2,000 suggested elicitation questions and a tested framework to help individuals make their project work more efficiently and effectively. She has been involved in the Information Technology (IT) industry since 1984 and founded Requirements Quest® in 2001. Roxanne earned a bachelor's degree in Management Information Systems (MIS) at the University of Wisconsin—Eau Claire, USA.

Roxanne's hard-won expertise, passion, and high-energy presentation style make her a popular and frequent speaker at business analysis industry conferences such as BusinessAnalystWorld. She delivers information-packed, practical advice and real world stories from her work with state universities, government agencies, and Fortune 500 enterprises spanning many industries.
To learn more about Roxanne or contact her, visit
http://www.requirementsquest.com/about-us/meet-roxanne.

Stakeholders and Change

"The only way to make sense out of change is to plunge into it, move with it, and join the dance." - Alan Watts

4

Know Your Stakeholders

Jonathan Nituch

We business analysts (BAs) consider ourselves to be in the "requirements business." Eliciting, managing, and communicating requirements take up most of our time. Doing a great job with those requirements is how we contribute value to our organizations. All this is true, but it is not how we *should* view ourselves. Business analysts are in the *stakeholder* business. Knowing your stakeholders in business analysis often means the difference between success and failure.

A BA often develops tricks to gather the requisite knowledge. For instance, in requirements workshops, I often pause to allow the stakeholders time to think. Some stakeholders don't always speak up quickly and need extra time to contribute. Those pauses pay off, and I can get many great requirements from pondering stakeholders.

However, I have also made mistakes. I have sometimes failed to identify the proper stakeholders, or failed to analyze them properly. These oversights have delayed my progress and had a negative impact on my work.

I have learned the hard way that not knowing stakeholders, especially when you *think* you know them, can be disastrous. The system you designed may work flawlessly for years and users may give you positive—even stellar—performance reviews, but then you very publicly and embarrassingly fail to get support for your next generation enhancements. How could this situation arise? The project was a large enterprise analysis engagement in the supply chain domain. The result was a list of potential projects I sought approval for, but my lack of stakeholder knowledge ultimately resulted in failure. I was the lead business analyst for a supply-chain system; let's call it System X.

A large consumer packaged goods manufacturer had decided to outsource its distribution chain. To develop the distribution network, the manufacturer signed agreements with a few distributors, each assigned to a territory. As part of this agreement, the distributors all had to use System X to record the sales and deliveries of products. The manufacturer agreed to pay for the costs of System X. These costs included all hosting, software, and hardware costs; and BA, QA, and support costs. A third-party vendor provided those services to maintain an arm's-length distance between the manufacturer and the distributors' data.

Competing Cultures, Needs and Expectations

I worked for the third-party vendor, whereas all users of System X worked for the distributors. This left System X strangely positioned, as the users and the owners were not from the same companies. Moreover, many of the distributors were new businesses; some were formed by former employees of the manufacturer to bid on the work their departments used to do. The whole purpose of the outsourcing project was to create strong, independent distributors who would stand on their own two feet and be good partners. The manufacturer considered System X "the distributors' system," because they were the primary users.

The variety of stakeholders made the job more challenging from a BA perspective; it also made it more fascinating and exciting! Inevitably, the big difference in cultures involved created differences in system needs and expectations. The manufacturer was a large multinational; the distributors were much smaller. Even within the distributors, much variety existed—some were family businesses, some were partnerships, and some were profit centers within corporations. Each territory was also very different in population and sales volume. Being in Canada, we also had different working languages.

Being a great BA involves being curious, and this environment had more than enough nuances to keep me engaged. The various companies each had different goals and different challenges, and I spent years working on System X and the associated businesses to understand them. I learned about the different processes the distributors put in place to approach their various territories. I saw the strategies and approaches they applied. The amazing aspect was how the distributors compared and contrasted. There were very few challenges any experienced alone; at the same time, very few issues affected them all.

After a few years, the new supply chain had matured nicely. The distributors operated well, and System X had a strong foundation of core capabilities. Around this time, the evolution of the distributors became a more prominent issue/concern. They grew in different ways. Many had new needs for System X, and more than one shared most of those needs.

Stakeholder Buy-in Vs. Showing Up

I decided to organize a user conference and obtain distributor support for my new ideas. I had several topics planned for the event; the main event was a portfolio management session on enhancements for

System X. I knew what all the distributors' pains were. I knew which capabilities System X was missing and I knew what kind of benefits the distributors could gain from the changes. I knew I could make a difference. There was business value to be had in these enhancements. I also knew which distributors would have an interest in various projects. By working together and splitting the costs, the distributors could achieve some very strong ROI. My plan was simple: I would get everyone in the same room and share the opportunities I had found. Several projects would be funded from this event—it was all very exciting!

The first lesson I will share with you is that getting all stakeholders to show up is not stakeholder buy-in. I managed to get all distributors to commit to the conference. Each group sent a delegation. Most delegations included a member of the distributor's ownership team and a key stakeholder who was involved with System X. I saw this as a clear win. System X was important enough for people to travel across the country to talk about it. This commitment was a sign that the distributors would be interested in investing, provided I could produce a clear business case. The manufacturer also agreed to send a delegation.

Before we go further, I want to share a side lesson—stick to what you know! If you are not an event planner, ask for help and focus your energy on your BA duties. Putting together the conference was a *lot* of work. A large part involved creating all the business cases; I had more than 20 projects of various sizes to present. For each one, I had worked with the appropriate stakeholders to understand the problem and the solution team to develop the implementation costs and timeline. It took months to prepare. The user conference was my idea, so besides the usual BA work, I also became the event planner. One distributor agreed to host, but I had much to coordinate and many documents and presentations to prepare.

My BA work was well in order, but all the details of the presentation and conference required I work the entire weekend putting the finishing touches on everything for Monday's conference. Anyone who has run any type of event can tell you that *run* is a good word for it. I was methodically running from one detail to another.

But, I did it! When I handed out the business cases to the stakeholders, my boss gave me a big smile and nod to let me know he was impressed. I had all the people in the same room and all the necessary information ready for them to make the right decision. We would make the system and the businesses better. I felt terrific. It would happen!

Know Thy Stakeholders - Asking the Right Questions

It didn't happen. The portfolio management session was almost a total flop. Of the 20-plus projects, a total of three were approved: two were very small expenditures, and one was paid for entirely by the manufacturer.

What happened? It was a tough pill to swallow. All the work I did turned into nothing. It took me a long time to understand what went wrong and why it was my fault. I didn't know my stakeholders. I had asked many of the *right* questions:

- What challenges is your business facing?
- What parts of System X frustrate you?
- What obstacles are preventing your business from growing?

I had done all the analysis to discover how the distributors could work together to solve these problems. I knew they were investing in other areas of their businesses. Why should System X be any different? There was one simple reason: they didn't *own* System X.

The questions I *should* have asked were:

- How do you feel about System X in general?

- Do you consider System X to be an asset in your business?
- Is System X part of your strategic plan?
- Do you have a sense of ownership or control over System X?

Those questions would have taken me directly to a basic conclusion—my stakeholders would never have invested in System X. System X was mandated on them; it wasn't *theirs*. They had no overall control over System X; the manufacturer could choose to replace it anytime. Furthermore, by investing in System X, the distributors would have taken on more ownership of the system, which could have left them open to assuming responsibility for the ongoing costs in future negotiations with the manufacturer. In short, investing in System X was a very bad idea for my stakeholders.

My stakeholders found an effective way to get more from the manufacturer—complaining about System X. This was the answer to the entire puzzle. Why did the distributors travel across the country to the user conference? Not to invest, but to complain. It was *their* chance to have everyone in the same room, to have all distributors and the vendor complain together to the manufacturer. The more the distributors complained about System X, the more likely the manufacturer was to invest its money in the system. Strategically, the distributors knew the best way to get anything done with System X— to complain.

I had become a pawn in that political process—a major vulnerability of the BA middleman. I gave substance and structure to those complaints. Every business case I presented was an argument that System X was not a fit and did not meet their needs. Meeting their needs was something System X was supposed to do, and fulfilling them was something the manufacturer had to pay for. The distributors weren't as interested in these improvements as they were in gathering ammunition for their negotiations with the manufacturer.

Knowing your stakeholders goes beyond the information available on the surface. You have to understand their positions and motivations.

Sometimes these might not be provided directly or explicitly, and you might have to dig more deeply and ask more questions. Understanding your stakeholders and their needs allows you to develop the best solutions possible, and it could save you many unnecessary headaches. In this case, I clearly failed. Learn from my mistake; know your stakeholders or your efforts will be wasted!

Jonathan Nituch
Fortress Technology Planners Inc.
Bankers Hall
PO Box 22415
Calgary, AB
T2P 5G7 Canada
T 403-274-3657 (114)
E-mail: jnituch@ftpinc.ca
Website: www.ftpinc.ca

Jonathan Nituch is the EVP of Fortress Technology Planners, a leading Canadian IT solutions provider. He has more than 18 years of experience in the technology and business fields. Jonathan's extensive consulting experience has allowed him to perform business analysis for small, medium, and large companies. This experience includes engagements in the distribution, finance, consumer packaged goods, oil and gas, facilities, food, and service industries.

Jonathan is a passionate member of the business analysis community. He contributes webinars, blogs, and articles to many organizations, including the IIBA and PMI. Jonathan is known for his passionate and engaging public speaking. His speaking appearances include the University of Calgary, Southern Alberta Institute of Technology, itSMF Southern Alberta Branch, and IIBA Calgary

Chapter.

Jonathan is the program coordinator for the business analysis certificate at Sheridan College. The certificate program is available in class and online. He has taught business analysis and project management at several Canadian postsecondary institutions. He has also developed several BA courses. Sharing his knowledge and experience with students is Jonathan's favorite way to give back to the BA community.

Jonathan holds a CBAP, PMP, and ITIL designation, and completed a BSc in Electronics Engineering Technology. He is a lifelong learner and continues to explore new topics. He lives in Calgary, Alberta, with his lovely wife Kerri.

5

Walk in Their Shoes

Rod MacPherson

My biggest problem with the business analyst (BA) community is the tendency for analysts to spend too much time worrying about what is important—that is, the business. They express this concern by capturing highly formalized requirements. I will suggest a slightly different approach—stepping into the clients shoes.

The typically diligent BA ensures the requirements template is designed, and the requirements gathering process properly becomes the focus of the project. It is typically planned in such a way to ensure all conceivable requirements are captured and perfectly documented. BAs are committed to excellence. The thorough requirements process reflects that. What's concerning about this scenario is that the BA is typically a consultant who hasn't worked for the organization and doesn't know anything about the business. It's not that they don't care; they just don't understand.

Aping the Client

This all happens before a single line of code is developed. The developer understands how to code functionality very well, but usually doesn't identify with the business, and as such, doesn't usually think the way the BA thinks. Developers think in the context of program/control logic.

The result? The developer creates elegant code that functions exactly how the BA thought the user wanted, and reflects the BA's commitment to providing a complete and accurate solution. When the solution is presented to the user team for testing however, it is realized that the BA, who didn't understand the business in the first place, has missed some important, but basic, concepts.

Some examples:

- If you are an accountant, debits always have to equal credits, and reconciling to the penny is the ultimate thrill, but materiality is king.
- If you are a lifeguard, your job is 99 percent about paying attention to the pool, and hopefully, even less than 1 percent about ever having to jump in the water to save someone.
- If you are a carpenter, you strive for perfection in your work, but your house is in disrepair.

People are passionate about their jobs, and only those people in the job understand what is needed and what will make their jobs easier. In my experience, I have worked with fantastic BAs who embrace the passion and standards of the profession and meticulously try to capture requirements. I have also worked with the not-so fantastic BAs—the ones who try to capture with perfection exactly what the user asks for, documenting every word he or she speaks, without taking the time to consider if it makes sense and without understanding the true meaning of the words spoken.

Stepping into the Client's Shoes

Brilliant BAs become surrogate experts in the business processes and requirements they capture. Although they may not share the passion, they come to understand what is important to the user. Once they achieve this understanding, they become the universal translators of IT, and they safeguard the user. If they have done their job right, user acceptance testing goes off without a hitch because the BAs have already tested the system and confirmed to IT that this is exactly what the user needs, and even more important, wants.

The innovative tactic you can use to achieve this performance? Rather than spending 30 days interviewing 15 people and writing results, divert at least half those days to doing the client's job, even if with bogus data. Walking in their shoes is the only way to understand their pain points and effectively define the opportunity to fix them.

Rod MacPherson, CMA
President, dCentricity Inc.
E-mail: rod@rodmacpherson.com
Twitter: @dcentricity

Rod is a consultant with more than 25 years of experience in finance, strategic planning, and data management. His background is finance; however, he transitioned from a functional to a technical role before launching his company, so he understands the dynamics from business requirements to developed solutions. As a professional accountant active internationally with the Data Management Association, he also understands the best practices from both perspectives.

6
Multicultural Challenges

Christine Beaulieu

Have you ever been called to work on a project already well under way, only to find challenging problems with the team members rather than with the project requirements themselves? Team members who refuse to communicate are scattered over three continents and making no efforts to achieve expected goals. Does this scenario sound familiar?

The first questions to come to mind are probably:

1. Why me?
2. Where do I start?
3. How do I get the requirements back on track?

After initial feelings of doubt, apprehension, and incomprehension, you realize the conflicts at hand stem from obvious cultural differences which have been overlooked by management.

The New Reality

Internationalization has opened global markets, created access to workforces worldwide, allowed the sharing of knowledge, promoted international communication technology, and opened the door to a whole array of exchange opportunities. As beneficial as this trend is, it has also brought cultural challenges. Since cultural diversity has made the management of work teams more complex, greater adaptability is required from business analysts. As business analyst, your role is to link these culturally diverse stakeholders by creating an opportunity to demystify and deal with both individual and common needs. As a moderator, the business analyst must be flexible to adapt to various situations and agile when managing human resources.

Creating Cultural Corridors

To manage cultural differences, you need to embrace flexible management practices that lead to the creation of "cultural corridors" where people, symbols, and common values transit. The lack of knowledge surrounding these corridors introduces challenges (such as …). Ignoring one group or many groups' cultural behaviors can potentially be catastrophic. Thus, it is crucial to understand and deal with these behaviors.

What's more, cultural differences are not limited to individual countries; they can be specific to a particular region, organization, and even generation. Recognizing these nuances is critical to not only detect and deal with potential conflicts, but also to better prepare when planning international negotiations. The primary objective of a successful business analyst is to develop a cohesive and harmonious team.

Background

As senior manager of a Quebec company, I was responsible for streamlining business practices at both the IT and operational levels. Two international European-based companies, one located in France and the other in England, owned the organization.

For several years, I was in charge of several projects involving team members from Europe, North Africa, and Canada, which led me to develop efficient methods for managing cultural diversity. But it would have been wrong to assume that working exclusively in Canada would be less challenging. The Anglo-Saxon approach is very different from say, the Latin, or other types of approaches. Many studies (try to?) compartmentalize cultures into continents and subdivide them into local groups.

Common Misconceptions

Despite the growth in globalization, many fallacies still dominate cultural management practices in organizations.

- I will impose my values, and others will follow suit.

The belief that we can change other people's values is misguided, especially when it comes to those values deeply rooted within our culture and ourselves. According to Geert Hofstede's "cultural onion," a person's culture is made of layers, at the very core of which reside his or her values.

- They'll get used to it!

The gap between cultural differences cannot be bridged with time. When it comes to values, people adjust rather than change. They may behave in the way you have asked them to, but they still believe in their values and rely on their cultural references.

Tips and Tricks

Here are a few useful tips when managing intercultural diversity. These tools and suggestions are provided only as guidelines. The concept of *one size fits all* does not apply to intercultural management. However, throughout the years, I have experimented with several strategies, and these guidelines have proven useful.

A. The Team Charter has been an indispensable tool. This tool allows you to minimize discomforts while targeting and streamlining business practices. The Charter also helps to improve the relationship among collaborators. Here are the basic principles a Team Charter should address.

> a. Strengths and weaknesses of each team member
>> i. We should list our strengths as a team and be able to honestly identify areas of improvement.
>
> b. Goals and objectives
> c. The values the team wishes to communicate
>> i. These values need to be understood, shared, and upheld.
>>> 1. Integrity, efficiency, collective recognition, and so on
>
> d. The various constraints the team will need to overcome
>> i. These constraints can include distance and time zones
>> ii. The various experiences of each team member
>
> e. Preferred means of communication
>> i. Technological tools
>>> 1. Virtual meetings
>>> 2. Collaboration tools
>> ii. Frequency of meetings and individual responsibilities
>
> f. Decision-making process to be implemented
> g. Strategies to resolve potential conflicts
> h. Escalation process to apply
> i. Others as needed

The Team Charter establishes work guidelines and is a reference document to guide each team member's behavior regardless of cultural nuances. The charter should be a collaborative effort. It is therefore important to the harmony of the group for each team member to create and approve its contents.

B. Using a Responsibility Assignment Matrix (RAM) Applying a RACI Format is indispensable to ensure that team members are accountable for their work. Without this tool, responsibilities can go astray, which can hamper the progress of activities and tasks. The acronym RACI is internationally recognized and can therefore be introduced easily into the project strategy. It is important to define and understand what each letter refers to to avoid any confusion about individual responsibilities.

R (responsible) refers to those responsible for carrying out a particular task. A (accountable) refers to the person ultimately accountable for approving and supervising the completion of a task. C (consulted) refers to those consulted during the activity. Finally, I (informed) refers to those who are informed of the progress of a task or activity.

Designing this type of matrix should be one of the first tasks on a business analyst's agenda, regardless of multicultural challenges. The matrix should not be a personal guideline for the analyst; it should be shared with and approved by all team members to ensure everyone's responsibilities are understood.

Deliverables	Stakeholder 1	Stakeholder 2	Stakeholder 3	Stakeholder 4	Stakeholder 5
		C	R		A
Deliverable 1		C	R	I	A
Deliverable 2		A	R		A
Deliverable 3		A			
Deliverable 4	C	A	R	C	C
Deliverable 5		R	C		A
Deliverable 6		R	C	I	A
Deliverable 7		A	R		C
Deliverable 8		A	R		C

R]esponsible   [A]ccountable   [C]onsulted   [I]nformed

FIGURE 3. Sample RACI Matrix

C. The Stakeholder Matrix is an essential tool for identifying influential team members in the framework of a project. Correctly positioning each stakeholder in this matrix is an important step in putting a strategy in place. In a multicultural context, it is especially important to identify the position of each "player" correctly. Does he or she have a high level of influence over the others, or is he or she mostly acting as a follower?

The grid can be made public, although you have to be careful not to create misunderstandings in your stakeholder community. This tool will help you as a business analyst minimize problems in your relationships with others. The benefits are the ability to better understand the influence and interests of your stakeholders, and manage your communication channels. As a "living matrix," it could change over time.

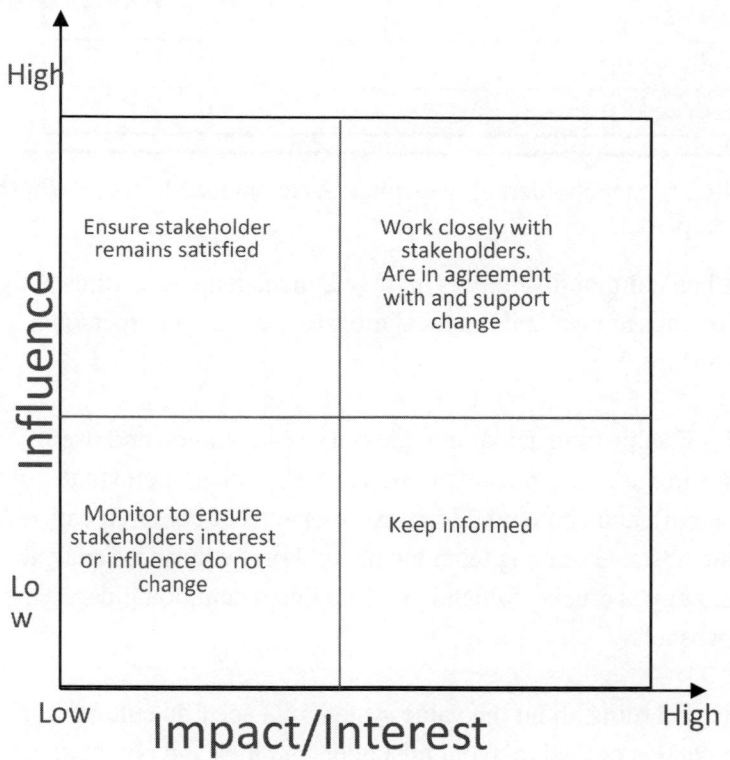

FIGURE 4. Stakeholder Matrix (*BABOK* Version 2.0, p. 30)

D. A Stakeholder's Engagement Assessment Matrix is also available. The PMI (Project Management Institute) included this matrix in the latest version of the *PMBOK*, reasserting the importance of identifying and positioning each stakeholder in a project's framework. The business analyst who works closely with various stakeholders should use this engagement assessment matrix to ensure the collaboration of each team member in the present and future. When cultural diversity is involved, management requires a high level of engagement and the use of crucial practical tools to facilitate interpersonal relationships. This matrix helps to fill out the roles and responsibilities grid and encourages the active participation of each team member.

Stakeholder	Unaware	Resistant	Neutral	Supportive	Leading
Stakeholder 1	C			D	
Stakeholder 2			C	D	
Stakeholder 3				D C	

FIGURE 5. Stakeholders Engagement Assessment Matrix (*PMBOK*, 5th Ed., p. 403)

When cultural diversity is involved, management requires a high level of engagement and practical tools to facilitate interpersonal relationships.

E.   Establishing a common glossary is a common and useful practice in multicultural situations. Textual (verbal), cotextual (nonverbal), and contextual (context) elements of communications can become obstacles among team members. For the business analyst, terminology is crucial, which is why having a common glossary is indispensable.

F.   Learning about the value system of a specific culture beforehand is critical to avoid misunderstandings and potential conflicts.

  a.   How to give out a business card
       Chinese people always give their business card using both hands as a sign of respect. To do otherwise is considered a lack of consideration towards others.
  b.   Is there an established procedure? Should I plan a meeting with the person?
  c.   How do you greet each other?
  d.   Does agreeing with a statement necessarily mean yes?
  e.   The sharing of knowledge and information might be

very different from what you are used to.

f. The concept of responsibility is not the same for everyone.

g. Courtesy expressions

G. Understanding the labor laws and regulations of each country involved. These can vary significantly by region and affect your engagements and target schedule. You sometimes will need to be creative when juggling conflicting holidays. The working conditions of one country may seem unfair to other team members and create conflicts.

H. Reading expert literature on management in multicultural contexts. Geert Hofstede is one of the best-known authors on the subject. He provides an in-depth look at six cultural dimensions to better understand the behaviors behind power and decision making. His works give a comprehensive overview of a wide variety of cultures worldwide while raising awareness of cultural differences so we can recognize them and respect them. However, we must be careful not to generalize. Every culture is unique to the people who make it up, along with their specific personalities and behaviors.

I. Finally, reading about the history and origins of the countries you will be working with can teach you much about their past, culture, allies, roots, and values. Has the country been conquered, or was it rather a conqueror? I remember working with a company that had multiple subsidiaries around the world. Its Trinidad and Tobago offices employed people from all over Europe, Asia, and Africa. Once a month, the company organized a dinner where employees took turns sharing their regional cuisine with their colleagues. These special events were always a great opportunity to share and discover new cultures, and greeted with much enthusiasm by the employees.

This cultural information allows us to position ourselves better and understand certain behaviors. It is more difficult to work in a country if we know little about its history. Showing interest in learning about another culture is a great sign of respect.

Conclusion

Cultural diversity will always be a challenge for the business analyst; however, as an agent of change, you should ensure that your style of leadership is adaptable. Situational or contextual leadership is a great advantage when dealing with intercultural work environments. Because of his remarkably curious personality, the business analyst is the perfect candidate for learning about and understanding his teammates, not by having to "decode" their behaviors, but by examining the foundations of these behaviors while making sure everyone is on the same page.

Cultural diversity in the workplace is enriching. We should learn to recognize the learning potential of these experiences to become key players in this ever-changing multicultural world.

References
Brennan, Kevin. *A Guide to the Business Analysis Body of Knowledge (BABOK Guide)*. Version 2.0 ed. Toronto: International Institute of Business Analysis, 2009. Print.

Davel, Eduardo, Dupuis, Jean-Pierre, Chanlat, Jean-François, eds. *Gestion en Contexte Interculturel*. Quebec: Les Presses de l'Université Laval et Télé-Université (UQAM), 2008.

Hofstede, G., Hofstede, G. J., Minkov, M. *Cultures and Organizations, Software of the Mind*: *Intercultural Cooperation and Its Importance for Survival*. New York, NY: McGraw Hill, 2010.

A Guide to the Project Management Body of Knowledge: (PMBOK® Guide). 5th ed. Newtown Square, Pa.: Project Management Institute, 2013. Print.

Christine Beaulieu
President, Gestion Christine Beaulieu Inc.
M 514 946-7507
E-mail: beaulieu.christine@sympatico.ca
Website: www.christinebeaulieu.com

Christine Beaulieu is an experienced information technology executive with more than 30 years of expertise. She is known for her management skills, and particularly for a managerial approach that rallies teams around projects of different size and scope.

Christine is the program director for the Business Analysis and Project Management certificate in Quebec. She is very involved in her community and efforts to raise the business analysis profession to a high level of competency. She acts as a senior consultant in business analysis coaching, change management, and business process review.

As a trainer and speaker, Christine specializes in the human aspects and communication in project management.

7

Working With Head, Heart, and Hand

David Rawsthorne

Delivering Sustainable and Meaningful Change

Have you ever worked on a project that delivered on time, to scope, and within budget, yet there was little enthusiasm or delight from the stakeholders in the weeks after implementation? Or on a change program in which end users bypassed the sophisticated new computer system, despite senior management hailing it as a resounding triumph?

Successful Failures

I like to call such projects "successful failures," and over the years, I've been involved in many. The key lesson I've learned to combat successful failures, and thus deliver meaningful sustainable change, is to engage stakeholders with holistic awareness of what they think

(Head), feel (Heart), and do (Hand). All too often as business analysts, we are stuck in our heads, thinking analytically with little consideration for how the finished product will be used and how consumers might feel about it.

Circumventing the System

I remember working at an insurance company where we implemented a new workflow system in which paper claim forms were scanned and automatically allocated to assessors. Several weeks after the go-live date, I was in the canteen when one of the claims team sat next to me and said, "Hi, David, you know we're not really using that new system you implemented. We simply don't work that way." I resisted the temptation to say that the requirements had been signed off, the scope delivered, and the sponsor was delighted. Clearly, something had gone wrong.

It turned out the staff wanted to be able to swap cases with colleagues who were better qualified to handle a particular claim. Fortunately, it was possible to make some minor tweaks that allowed claims to be transferred from one assessor to another, if both agreed. And the team loved the change; it fit their culture of working collaboratively and flexibly. Success, finally!

Head, Heart, and Hand

Around the same time I was working on this project, I was training to be a yoga teacher. A key concept in yogic philosophy is the integration and balancing of Head (thinking and structure), Heart (feeling and culture), and Hand (doing and change). These are three aspects of every person; you don't need to be a psychologist or yoga teacher to understand the concept.

In the above example, I hadn't appreciated the Heart of the end users; the claims allocation process didn't align with assessors' culture of collaborating. An unplanned conversation brought about a more harmonious way of working. I wondered if the concept of Head, Heart, and Hand could be applied more consciously to business analysis or more broadly across a project or program. It didn't take long to come up with a simple model.

Table 1: The Head, Heart and Hand Business Analysis Model

	Is about	Typical project fit	When it goes wrong
Head thinking ☺	STRUCTURE ✓ Developing and testing concepts ✓ Logic, process, measurement	» Business Analyst	✗ Loss of clarity and original intent ✗ Unnecessary detail ✗ Loss of meaning
Heart feeling ♥	CULTURE ✓ Having a sense of connectedness ✓ Harmony, balance, unity	» Sponsor » End user	✗ Personal conflict, fear of change ✗ Disagreement within the group ✗ Loss of culture & identity
Hand doing 🖐	CHANGE ✓ Directing towards a common goal ✓ Actions, outputs, outcomes	» Project Manager	✗ Anarchy or dictatorship ✗ Uncontrolled change ✗ Loss of context

Project Team Imbalance and Dysfunction

There's a natural fit between project roles and the Head, Heart, and Hand model, and therein lies a key cause of *successful failures*. Project teams are commonly created with much effort spent on having a balanced team structure (the number of business analysts, developers, and testers) and a range of technical competencies. Putting a different lens over the team reveals plenty of scope for imbalance and dysfunction:

The Business Analyst (Head) focuses on process, logic, and structure. Over analyzing can lead to unnecessary detail and forgetting the original reason for delivering.

The Project Sponsor (Heart) might be more concerned with looking good in front of his or her peers and using emotional blackmail to drive delivery; anger or wide-eyed optimism is common when the sponsor and project team do not work collaboratively.

The Project Manager (Hand) might be focused on scope, budget, and timelines to the detriment of sustainable change. Simply getting a project delivered is no guarantee that a few weeks later its deliverables will be used as intended, or even used.

Delivering Requirements With Head, Heart, and Hand

Business analysts are logical humans, yet not always concerned whether requirements can be delivered (we can leave this to the project manager) or sustained after implementation (the sponsor can deal with that). We learn the theory and definition of requirement attributes and categories, for example, functional as opposed to nonfunctional requirements. This approach is far too logical, and it can fail spectacularly when we have to present our work for approval and signoff.

I've discovered from direct experience that overlaying the qualities of Head, Heart, and Hand helps to distill requirements which deal with human aspects and gain genuine commitment from stakeholders. Here are some questions I ask during requirements elicitation; they have a natural flavor of Head (thinking), Heart (feeling), or Hand (doing), as do the requirements they elicit. We'll come back to this shortly.

Table 2: Requirements Elicitation Questions

Head thinking ☺	What do you think about this requirement? Is it logical and consistent with other requirements? Does it form part of a larger process or logical sequence? Does it depend on any other requirements? How would you test or verify this requirement?
Heart feeling ♥	How do you feel about this requirement? How would this affect your role and job satisfaction? How does this fit with the culture, and the way things are done around here? How would customers feel about doing things this way? Does it improve their experience?
Hand doing ✋	Is this requirement practicable? Could you implement it? And how would you implement it? How would this requirement work in the daily operation of the business? Does it change overall handling/process times? Does it make things simpler?

You could use an analogous set of questions to support other business analysis tasks, such as process mapping or usability. I'll leave you to devise your way of applying Head, Heart, and Hand to other tasks.

A Practical Roadmap

There is no guarantee, but as a curious business analyst, wouldn't you want to try out a new tool that could improve your chances of success? Here is a simple, practical roadmap you can use to put Head, Heart, and Hand into action.

Table 3: Head, Heart and Hand Action Roadmap

Be aware of your natural inclinations and tendencies.

Are you naturally more inclined to thinking, feeling, or doing?

Rate yourself by putting an 'X' somewhere between No and Yes on each line below. It's not supposed to be scientific, simply an indicator of your inclinations.

Do this quickly and honestly.

No ------ Yes I tend to think/be analytical (Head)

No ------- Yes I tend to feel/be emotive (Heart)

No ------- Yes I tend to do/be dynamic (Hand)

See if your work reflects your natural inclinations.
Check for balance among Head, Heart, and Hand.

Print a set of requirements you've written recently. Take a colored pen, and without thinking too hard, quickly draw a head, heart, or hand next to each requirement. The previous section on requirements elicitation will give you some tips on how to do this.

Now, flick through the annotated document and see if any patterns emerge:

> Can your beautifully chosen words (Head) be implemented in practice (Hand)?
> Do your requirements, especially the nonfunctional ones, capture the cultural and emotional aspects that will engage your sponsor, end users, and customers? (Heart) Applying Head, Heart, and Hand in retrospect, what would you like to change in these requirements?

If you have a good balance, then it's much more likely that you have engaged your stakeholders, and they will support and promote the requirements and associated changes you have documented.

Think about your colleagues, team, and community—what are their natural inclinations and tendencies?	Look impartially around your colleagues, team, and community: Do you see roles reflecting natural tendencies, or are there some team members who have a more balanced Head, Heart, and Hand? Does the team as a whole tend towards Head, Heart, or Hand? Does the overall mix of thinking / feeling- / doing lead to harmony and balance?
Adapt your behavior to better connect or resonate within and beyond the team.	Make a conscious effort to balance your thoughts, feelings, and actions: Be mindful of your natural tendencies for logic, emotion, or action. Be aware in all your interactions of the interplay of Head, Heart, and Hand, both yours and those with whom you interact. Consciously engage with all three aspects of Head, Heart, and Hand, not just the one with which you are naturally most comfortable.
Observe the impact of your newfound awareness.	Imagine yourself as an impartial witness of this process. What difference (if any) does it make when you use this model? • Do you start to think differently? • Do you start to feel differently? • Do you start to act differently?

Share your experience. Choose a colleague whom you know and trust. Share that you are working with Head, Heart, and Hand. Be open and receptive to all his or her comments and feedback.

If you feel uncomfortable using these words, find another way to express it, for example, "looking at what we think, feel, and do to achieve better understanding and outcomes."

Context and Meaning

For a project to be meaningful, it needs an overall framework, as represented in the below illustration. To be sustainable, all those involved must have a shared desire to fulfill the project's intent during the project's lifetime and beyond implementation into business-as-usual applications.

Context sets out the organizational background, how the project came about, and where it fits. It's common for a business case to cover this, while totally missing the meaning of the project. Meaning deals with the effect project implementation will have on individuals (customers, end users, project sponsors, and community); Head, Heart, and Hand sits here.

Table 4: Defining Context and Meaning

CONTEXT (affecting the Organisation)
What is this project about?
Why are we doing it, where did it originate?
How does it fit into our universe?

MEANING (affecting Individuals)
Will I need to think in another way? What's in it for me?
(Head)

How will I feel? How will it affect the way I do things, and our culture? (Heart) What will I have to do differently? What changes will I have to make? (Hand)	
HEAD Thinking / Structure HEART Feelings / Culture HAND Doing / Change	BALANCE & HARMONY between Business Analyst, Project Manager, Sponsor, and the project community will lead to... SUSTAINABLE & MEANINGFUL CHANGE ...where everyone is genuinely engaged with Head, Heart and Hand. There will be a natural desire to sustain change and its benefits.

Over to You

By being able to understand and appreciate the simple power of Head, Heart, and Hand, you will be better equipped to deliver sustainable and meaningful change in your role as a business analyst, and more widely across your project team and community.

It really does work. Try it!

Business Analysis Book of Mentors

David Rawsthorne
Bank of New Zealand (New Zealand)
E-mail: nadarupa@me.com

Originally from Liverpool, David now calls Waiheke Island, New Zealand, home.
David has more than 25 years' experience in business analysis and management consultancy in the United Kingdom and New Zealand. He worked for many years with PriceWaterhouse management consultancy in London and with UK retail groups Kingfisher and Arcadia.

Besides having a Cambridge degree in mathematics, David spent a postgraduate year studying violin and viola performance at the Royal Academy of Music, London. In his spare time, you can find David running local yoga and meditation retreats and playing violin with his string quartet and jazz trio.

Accredited Teacher SATYANANDA YOGA® Academy 21419
British Wheel of Yoga Teaching Diploma (DipBWY)
M.A. (Cantab)

8

Creating Effective One-Page Documents to Establish Shared Understanding

Patrick van Abbema

There are too many examples of business analysts who failed to effectively create a shared and common understanding with stakeholders because they failed to understand the information needs of their audience. This article reviews how to analyze the information needs of your stakeholders and provides examples of how to create one-page documents to effectively communicate with them.

As a project team member, we all want to achieve the following outcomes:

- Reduce waste
- Create solutions
- Complete projects on time
- Improve efficiency
- Document the right requirements
- Identify the causes of problems

The question is how do we, as project team members, work with stakeholders to effectively set and manage their expectations? Let's first review factors that lead to failed outcomes due to poor communication on projects:

- Costly mistakes
- Poor compliance
- Failed or delayed audits
- Inefficiency (people, process, technology)
- High translation costs
- Ineffective documentation and/or training
- Poor quality/best practices
- Low customer satisfaction/high support costs
- Lack of standards
- Incomplete or expensive technology adoption
- Poor product knowledge

The 7 Cs of Communication

How can we reduce the probability of these poor results on a project? Answer: By improving our communication skills. You can improve your communication skills by applying the 7 Cs of communication design. The seven Cs lay out a simple sequence that can help you start broadly and work your way down to specifics.

Let's review the seven Cs in order:

1. Context

What's going on? Do you understand the situation? Is there an elephant in the middle of the room? Ask good questions. You'll need a clear goal before you begin to design any communication. Ask: To whom are you talking, and what do you want them to do?

2. Content

Based on your goal, define a single question that your communication is designed to answer. This is the best possible measure of communication effectiveness. What do you want your audience to walk away with and remember? Once you have defined your prime question, set out to answer it. What information is required? Do you have the answer already, or do you need to search it out?

3. Components

Before you build anything, break your content into basic *building blocks* of content. Formulate the information into clusters and groups. What patterns emerge? How can you make the information modular? Given your goal, what is the most basic unit of information? Use index cards to break information into modules.

4. Cuts

This is one of the most difficult parts of the process and most often neglected. Your client's attention will quickly drift—she expects you to get to the point and not waste her time. Learn to edit and stay on point.

5. Composition

Now, it's time to design the way you will tell your story. Draw on both written and visual composition. When writing, who are your main characters? How will you set the scene? What goals and conflicts will develop? How will the story reach resolution? In visual terms, where will the reader begin? How will you lead the eye around the page? In all your compositional thinking, how will you engage your audience? How will you keep them engaged? Writing it down forces you to think through it.

6. Contrast

What differences matter? Use contrast to highlight them: big as opposed to little, rough as opposed to smooth, black as opposed to white. When making any point, ask, "in comparison with what?" Contrast is a trigger to the brain that says, "Pay attention!"

7. Consistency

Unless you're highlighting differences, keep visual elements such as color, fonts, spacing, and type sizes consistent to avoid distracting the reader. Any extraneous information detracts from the ability to assimilate and learn.

Depending at what point in the project life cycle you've used this technique, you'll have different next steps. For example, if you are helping to construct the project or business problem statement, you'll want to document the related objectives and business needs of the project. Alternatively, if you are evaluating the cause of a defect or bug, you'll want to communicate your findings to the solution developers so they can adjust appropriately. Share the results of the cause analysis with those affected by the problem or solution. Communication modes could include:

-Formal documents
-E-mail
-Agile scrums or other team meetings
When designing communication documents for your stakeholders, remember to keep in mind the 7 Cs of communication.

Communicating With One-page Documents

How do I effectively communicate with stakeholders using one-page documents? Anyone can easily complicate situations with poorly written and lengthy communication documents (for example, a 30-plus page communication strategy). The key to successful communication is to make complicated situations simple to understand and digest for your intended audience. Start with the following questions when creating communication articles:

-Who is the intended audience?
-Why do they want to know this information?
-Where are they located?
-What is the message?
-When does this message need to be delivered?
-How will you deliver this message?

Knowing your audience's information needs will help you communicate more effectively. Let's review the below example of using one-page documents to communicate with your audience.

Example #1—One-page business case

Who—Executive stakeholders

Why—Need a yes/no decision to move forward with the project

Where—Different offices across the country

What—Highlight key points of the business case

When—Next steering committee

How—High-level summary document will be sent ahead of meeting for executives to review

(A detailed business case is available on request.)

A typical business case can be several pages in length (for example, 20-plus pages), but if you wanted to create a summary of the business case so all stakeholders could easily read and understand it, then you would create a one-page overview of the document. See below example (Figure 1):

Business Case for Project <CODE> : <Project Name>		
Brief overview about the project>	Executive Sponsor :	Project Category

Business Drivers

☒ To meet other mandatory requirements

<Organization> Priorities

☒ Infrastructure Enhancements

Expected Benefits

√fully supported, and industry, partner and user interoperability level for the next 3 or so years.

Options/Recommendation

The only option other than the proposed upgrade is to maintain status quo …

Business Impact

IM/IT will work closely with the business units to test compatibility of all currently supported applications and offer a remediation plan for applications that cannot be made compatible with the new platform. Remediation of unsupported applications and user developed local tools is outside the scope of this project. IM/IT will provide access to lab environments for business users to test and verify compliance of applications and local tools not supported by IM/IT.

Project Cost

		One Time Implementation			Recurring year	TCO (5 years)
	Project Costs	FY2010-11	FY2011-12	Total One-time		
	Internal					
	Labour	$40,000	$85,250	$125,250		
IM/IT	External					
	Labour	$200,000	$341,917	$541,917		
	IM/IT Total	$240,000	$427,167	$667,167		
	Internal					
	Testing	$0.00	$121,500	$121,500		
	Training	$0.00	$375,000	$375,000		
	External					
BU	Testing	$0.00	$22,500	$22,500		
	BU Total	$0.00	$519,000.00	$519,000.00		
TOTAL		$240,000	$946,167	$1,186,167	$1.4M *	$2.586M @

There are no Incremental recurring costs. @ Staff training is budgeted at $375K in Annual Training Plan. Training package (coach + materials) will be outsourced to an external training provider, therefore included in the project cost estimate.

Project Risks and Mitigation

Risk	Mitigation
User resistance to move to new platform	Project will engage an "Organization Change Manager" to plan for and address user concerns through communication, training and support.

Project Milestones

ID	Task Name	Start	Finish	Duration	Q2 11	Q3 11
					Mar Apr May Jun	Jul Aug Se
	TESTING - Iterative approach	07/05/2011	02/04/2011	16w		
	PILOT - Iterative approach	02/07/2011	16/08/2011	20w		
	PRODUCTION DEPLOYMENT - Iterative approach	30/05/2011	30/09/2011	12w		

Windows 7 operating system will be deployed to approximately 85% (based on Industry best practices) Training/migration is scheduled for each

FIGURE 1: One-page Document Example

Identifying Stakeholder Needs

Example #2—Test case template (used to verify a use case)
  Who—Project stakeholders
  Why—Need to communicate the results to all stakeholders on a
  project
  Where—Different offices across the country
  What—Highlight key points of the test case
  When—Present during testing report summary
  How—High-level summary document will be sent ahead of
  meeting for project team members to review
  NB—Several great tools can help capture and report test results.

This is intended for an audience without access to these tools.

Description	Verification that <product shall…>				
Scenario#	<1000x				
Step #	Description	Procedure	Expected Results	Actual Results	Pass/ Fail
1					
2					
3					
4					
5					
6					

FIGURE 2: Test Case Template

Understanding the information needs of your stakeholders is an
important part of a project's successful outcome. The stakeholders'
needs will have to be correctly interpreted and communicated
effectively. Different stakeholders perceive the same problem
differently, depending on whether they are at the executive, functional,
or operational level. They might need different information, and it is
your role, as a project team member, to understand their information

needs and communicate *effectively* to these different stakeholders.

Patrick van Abbema, PMP, CBAP, CSP
Senior Project Advisor/Chief Business Analyst
AltNexus Corporation
M 613-316-3244 F 866-314-7916
Twitter: @pvanabbema
Website: http://www.AltNexus.com
LinkedIn: http://www.linkedin.com/in/pvanabbema

Patrick has more than 20 years of progressive accomplishments in competitive Digital Media, Web collaboration, and Enterprise/SaaS software markets. Patrick is the Senior Project Advisor and Chief Business Analyst for AltNexus Corp. and provides consulting expertise on enterprise service strategies for various public and private sector clients across the USA, Canada, and Europe. He is responsible for analyzing the business needs of his clients and acts as a liaison among stakeholders to elicit, analyze, communicate, and validate requirements for changes to business processes, policies, and information systems. He recommends solutions that enable organizations to achieve their business goals.

Patrick is also known in the industry for his innovative approaches to solving common project management problems. He focuses on two project management specialty areas: agile project management and troubled project recovery. He delivers several workshops on Agile and Enterprise Analysis to universities across Canada.

9

The Business
Therapist

Mike Crawford

Lessons from Psychotherapy

Business analysis has much more in common with psychotherapy than our clients would suspect. Psychotherapists avoid telling clients what their problems are or how to fix them. Almost no one takes that kind of advice, anyway. Therefore, therapists ask questions and make observations to guide patients towards understanding and dealing with their difficulties.

To ask effective questions, psychotherapists work from models that have proved successful in the past. These models (Gestalt, Cognitive Behavioral Therapy, Narrative, and so on) provide structures for exploring people's subjective experience. Similarly, business analysts (BAs) engage with business clients, asking questions that help identify and solve business problems. To ask effective questions, BAs use business analysis models (Value Chain Analysis, Business Model Canvas, Soft Systems Methodology, and many, many more) that provide ways to explore business problems and opportunities.

The difference between a therapist and a good therapist is how appropriately he chooses his questions and how skilled he is at noticing the implications of the answers he obtains, which is also true of BAs. One day, I'll write the business psychotherapy book. Until then, I hope this story helps illustrate why I view business analysis as a form of psychotherapy, and why I think it's a useful way to think about our work as BAs.

***

Analyzing the Client

I'd like to tell you I was doing something important and technical when Mick Mathews phoned me. Actually, I was making a paperclip sculpture, which is about as bored as a person can be without losing consciousness. Mick said a friend suggested I might be able to help him with a business problem. He didn't have time to talk now, but wondered whether I could visit him the following morning at nine. I said nine was fine and took the details. The company was Vital Signs, and the address was 17 Summer Road. Happily, Summer Road was less than a 15-minute walk from my office.

I hung up the phone and Googled Vital Signs for their website, all two pages. The homepage had a company banner, some description of the services offered (sign manufacture and fitting, along with a design service) and a link to the Contact Us page. The two "examples of our work" photos were less than inspiring, and the accompanying text took a somewhat cavalier approach to both the English language and punctuation. I began to suspect this was a one-man business, and the one man had no flair for marketing.

Therefore, as I walked along Summer Road the next morning, I was surprised to see that Vital Signs had its own small two-story office and a sizable adjoining industrial unit. Both were bright, clean, and modern, which didn't fit my one-man-band vision of the day before.

Reception was empty, so I pressed the button above the sign that read, "Press for Attention." A door behind the counter opened, and in walked what seemed to be a bear wearing engineer's overalls. It said, "Hi, I'm Mick Mathews," and offered me a hand the size of a baseball catcher's mitt. I shook it, and I was grateful to get my arm back. Mick suggested a guided tour of the workshop and coffee afterward. I would rather have talked first, but he had the demeanor of a man who made suggestions with which no one disagreed. I decided not to break that tradition.

Diagnosing a Dependency Problem

As we walked, I noticed a rack area stacked high with magazines. He told me it was storage for his other business—distributing specialist publications. Apparently, it was very successful, but he showed no great enthusiasm for it, and I gathered his wife and brother had control of the daily management. However, the signs business was very much his baby, and he proudly showed me layout tables, the metal sheets, plastic boards, rolls of vinyl in stock, cutters, printers, drills, and lathes; and a huge CNC flat-bed router to machine woods, plastics, and metals to fine tolerances. Computers and CAD/CAM systems, for designing signs and controlling the machinery, were in a purpose-built room close by. If none of this makes any sense to you, don't worry. In short, there was a whole bunch of highly sophisticated sign-making stuff.

What I didn't see was any activity, except for one man, Ted, repairing a damaged shop sign. I asked Mick how many people worked for him, and he said six full-time staff with some casual labor during high-demand periods. Apparently, the previous few weeks had been spent manufacturing nearly 30 signs for the midtown shopping mall, and everyone but Ted was outfitting them.

On the way back to the office, we came across a gleaming blue and gray 1966 Chevrolet Corvette Stingray. The Corvette is, perhaps, the iconic American sports car. I asked what it was doing there, and Mick said it was a wreck he'd been fixing. It turned out he had no formal training, but a natural talent for anything practical. He could build a house from foundation to roof, including bricklaying, electrical, plumbing, plastering, tiling, and carpentry. He repaired failed circuit boards in Vital Signs' computer controlled machinery, and he had rebuilt the Corvette's seized engine, rewelded the frame, restored the interior, and almost completed a full rewire.

Back in the office, we sat by the coffeemaker, and I asked what he wanted to talk about.

"I'm not really sure," he said. "I think the company should be doing a lot better. We have peaks and troughs. No work one month and then all rush jobs the next. I need a smoother workflow."

"Is it profitable?"

"Oh, yes. The materials for the signs in the mall cost me less than a grand, and I'm charging nearly five."

"Sounds good, but is it profitable? I imagine the wages and operating overheads with all that machinery must be a much larger proportion of the cost than materials."

It usually worries me when somebody says, "Don't worry about it," which is what Mick said. It got worse. He told me, "The magazine business pays the cost of the building and I own the machines, so it's only the wages to cover."

I said, "So your other business covers the overheads of this business. What happens if the other business hits hard times and can't subsidize Vital Signs?" His look clearly indicated that he didn't intend to discuss this subject any further, and he said firmly, "That won't happen."

Here's a man with two businesses. One makes a good profit, but he has no interest in it, and one clearly loses money, but he loves it because it uses his practical talents. He buys the machines because he likes them, not because the business needs them—boys and their toys. He's unwilling to discuss it because he knows there's no logical argument to support his case.

What's Your Weltanschaaung?

I needed some way to address the Vital Signs problem without implying personal criticism, which meant focusing solely on the company issues. I decided to pursue some avenues using CATWOE.

CATWOE comes from Soft Systems Methodology (SSM). SSM is particularly useful when stakeholders lack common agreement or a clear understanding of the business problems. CATWOE provides an incisive set of questions to explore client perceptions (perspectives) of the business they're in. It's not my intention here to describe CATWOE in detail, but it stands for Customers, Actors, Transformation, Weltanschauung, Owners, and Environment. It's standard practice to start with the Transformation and Weltanschauung.

The Transformation is what the enterprise does. Vital Signs designed, manufactured, and fitted signs.

The *Weltanschauung* (a German word that translates literally as "world view") relates to values, ethics, and emotions. For me, it's about the value of the Transformation, that is, my client's perception of the value he offers his customers.

So, a mortgage company might say it "helps people to buy their own homes," but what the company *does* is sell mortgages. The "help people..." is more a statement of the *value* of what they do; it's the Weltanschauung.

I would never ask, "What's your Weltanschaaung?" because, rightly, I'd be beaten to a pulp and thrown out the door for using jargon like that. Instead, I asked Mick why he was in this business, and he replied, "To make money." Now, that's not the answer I was looking for because it isn't about values. I don't ask questions randomly—they're specific questions to get specific answers, so I said, "Absolutely, but why choose signs to make money?" and he said, "People need signs." OK, now we're getting somewhere. I asked "Why?" and he replied, "When you came here today, how did you find this place?" I knew exactly what he meant. I'd walked up the road looking for the sign that read "Vital Signs."

"Not only do businesses need signs so people can find them, but the quality of those signs matters. High-quality signage creates an impression. We produce high-quality signage."

I'd been looking for this Weltanschaaung. Mick believed companies needed signs so their customers could find them, and high-quality signs added value to those companies. This made (business) sense of all that investment in the machinery.

Next, I asked Mick who his customers (the C in CATWOE) were. He said, "Mostly local businesses. They look at local listings and search online for this area. They want someone close by to go talk through ideas with and maybe see some designs. They're not sure what they want, but they want it quickly and cheaply. There's no point having a fancy website because they're not that interested."

I noticed his customers didn't match his perspective of the business. That's to say, he talked of the value of high-quality signs, but his clients didn't value high quality; they valued low cost. He said, "Yeah, you're right. I really hadn't noticed that before." This was why expensive machinery laid idle, losing money, most of the time. I didn't say that—he would have been defensive—so I said, "Maybe we could think of ways to get clients who do want high quality." He said, "Yeah, maybe."

The Diagnosis

With a few weeks' hard work, I identified some local companies that seemed like promising customers, created a first-cut plan to market to them, and prototyped some web pages to make the online presence look more credible in our new marketplace. I presented all this to Mick, and he said great, he'd look at it, add his thoughts, and get back to me. It never happened.

There seemed no good reason not to pursue my ideas. They were cheap to implement and, if successful, could have transformed his business. It drove me crazy for a while; then I remembered if someone isn't emotionally ready for a change, it doesn't matter how good the idea is or what the arguments in favor of it are; they simply won't run with it.

Later, an alternative strategy occurred to me. I'd found successful sign companies that couldn't offer such sophisticated products because they didn't have Vital Signs' level of technology. My thought was that we could provide high-tech services as subcontractors. I didn't say so, though. During a discussion, I merely observed that many sign makers would give their right arm for the capability Vital Signs had.

The next week, Mick said he'd had the idea to place an advert in a trade journal, offering high-end manufacturing to sign makers. He'd already had a few credible enquiries. I said, "Congratulations" and told him it was a brilliant idea. He proudly agreed. It was, in the end, how Vital Signs began to generate sustainable, predictable income.

So, what's the lesson? I guess it's this. Business analysis is about people. Businesses are made of people, so they behave like people, not always logically. They're frequently dazzled by bright, shiny baubles that promise a better world, but don't deliver, such as software packages that don't support their requirements because they never defined their requirements.

As analysts, we should be mindful that our clients, like us, have egos, neuroses, hidden agendas, strengths, and weaknesses. So, think before telling people the answers to their problems. If they're not ready to listen, use systematic questioning, observation, and analysis to help them discover their solutions—even if they're yours.

Mike Crawford
T +61 (0)2-8021-8844 M +61 433-765-531
E-mail: mike@mpc-cs.com
Twitter: @crawfordthinks
Skype: mpcrawford

Mike has been a systems and business analyst for 30 years. He's also been a programmer, designer, consultant, project manager, and company director. In 1986, he founded a UK software house and IT training company.

He moved to Sydney, Australia, in 2009, where he has engaged in various consultancy and training assignments as well as presenting sessions and workshops at industry events for organizations such as the Australian Computer Society, the IEEE, and the Business Analysis World Conferences.

He is currently Director of Business Analysis Services at Planit Software Testing (Australia) where he established the Business Analysis Services unit. He is the architect of Planit's Business Analysis Capability Framework, which encompasses BA processes, standards, competencies, skills, tools, and techniques.

Mike is a writer for the *IIBA's Guide to the BABOK*, Version 3, an examiner for the British Computer Society's International Business Analysis Diploma, and an accredited assessor for the Australian Institute of Business Analysis (AIBA). He is also a trained mediator (with Mediation UK) and NLP Master Practitioner.

Technology

"One machine can do the work of fifty ordinary men. No machine can do the work of one extraordinary man." - Elbert Hubbard

10

In Defense of Systems Analysis

Maria Amuchastegui

Why Business Analysts Should Stay Close to the Technical Side

My father was a systems analyst at IBM, so in a sense, I'm a second-generation business analyst. Many years ago, when I first moved into business analysis, my father advised me to stick close to the technical side. Good technical people, said my dad, are difficult to find, but business people are comparatively expendable. My dad wasn't advising me to remain a computer programmer, as rewarding as the career is. He was pleased I had solid written and spoken communication skills, which technical folks often lack. Rather, he argued that a business analyst (BA) who combines communication skills with a solid technical background would never be out of a job.

BAs add value because they stand at the intersection between business and IT. A skilled BA combines some skills of a project manager (PM), such as stakeholder and issue management, with some skills of a software developer or even a solutions architect, such as UML or data modeling. The BA's unique position at the juncture of business and IT is a strength, but it can also lead to ambiguity in role definition. The overlap in skillsets between BAs and PMs can be particularly troublesome because BAs often report to PMs.

Imagine a Venn diagram showing the skillsets of PMs, software developers, and BAs. The PM bubble would show skills that are the sole bailiwick of PMs, such as budgeting and scheduling, but it would also overlap with skills that PMs share with BAs, such as stakeholder engagement and requirements management. The software developer bubble would show hard-code technical stuff such as coding and infrastructure, but it would also overlap with skills that technical folks share with BAs, such as systems analysis and high-level design. The BA skillset bubble would encompass some PM skills (stakeholder engagement and requirements management) with some of the more technical skills (systems analysis and high-level design).

The BA's Competitive Advantage

One strategy for dealing with role ambiguity is to focus on those skills the other person doesn't have. An economist would call a skill held by only one of two competing entities a *competitive advantage*. For example, if a given country produces cheap textiles but expensive cars, then that country should focus on textiles and let other countries produce cars.

In a project management setting, a PM who considers it is his sole prerogative to engage with stakeholders may feel a BA who engages with stakeholders to elicit requirements is encroaching on his turf. To deal with such a PM, the BA might emphasize systems analysis or documentation skills—skills the PM is less likely to have. In this way, the BA can demonstrate that he or she adds value, while not encroaching on what the PM (falsely) believes to be his turf.

Technical Knowledge = Power

Another way of thinking about technical knowledge is as a source of power. Power can be derived from various sources: your job title, your ability to punish, your ability to reward, your charisma, the information you are privy to, and your expertise. As a rule of thumb, PMs have the first three types of power: (1) power derived from one's job title, also known as *positional or legitimate power*; (2) power derived from one's ability to punish, also known as *coercive power*; and (3) power derived from one's ability to reward, also known as *reward power*.

Both BAs and PMs can cultivate the other three kinds of power: (4) power derived from one's charisma or charm (*referent power*); (5) power derived from information (*information power*), which can be anything from organizational history to social gossip; and (6) power derived from expertise (*expert power*), including technical expertise.

Technical Knowledge = Money

Technical knowledge can also be a source of money, which is another reason BAs should focus on the technical side. If you put keywords such as "data modeling" on your CV, recruiters will fall over themselves to call you. If your CV lists only soft skills, not so much.

Technical Knowledge = Job Mobility

Technical skills can also be a way for a BA to move laterally from one industry to another. Many job descriptions for BA positions will say something such as "must have knowledge of UML and the insurance industry." If you have strong knowledge of UML, for instance, then the employer might disregard the fact that you don't have business knowledge of a particular industry. For me, being a technical BA has enabled me to have a career that spans government, healthcare, financial services, and telecommunications.

For many BAs, focusing on the technical side is also more suited to their personality. Business analysts tend to be, well, analytical, and as a rule of thumb, analytical types tend to be introverts. Not everyone has a need to seek the limelight by interacting with high-profile stakeholders. Some people might feel more comfortable drafting a technical specification or closely inspecting a file layout. And that's OK.

But the most compelling reason to stick to the technical side, for many BAs, is that they find it more interesting than the business side. I originally started to work in the IT sector because I found technology interesting, and not because I had an affinity for the corporate world. When I moved to a BA role, my programmer colleagues expressed dismay that I had moved to the *dark side*. Actually, this explains why some PMs insist on eliciting requirements from stakeholders; it's much more interesting than managing schedules and budgets.

Developing Technical Skills and Expertise

OK, you might say; I'm sold. I'd like to hone my technical BA skills because they will give me job security, lateral mobility, and possibly even money and power. What do I need to know? Well, you should learn traditional systems analysis skills—data flow diagrams (especially context diagrams), data modeling, and data dictionaries. You should be able to write a use case with your eyes closed, and you should learn UML (unified modeling language).

Two growth areas for BA jobs now are "business intelligence analyst" and "agile analyst." If you look closely at the job descriptions for those positions, they are systems analyst jobs. A business intelligence analyst is a systems analyst who works on business intelligence systems. Because a business intelligence system includes a relational database, BI analysts must know about data modeling and data dictionaries, besides understanding business needs. Similarly, an agile analyst is a systems analyst who works on agile software development projects. An agile analyst must be able to write user stories, which are conceptually similar to use cases, in addition to understanding business needs.

You might object—but I don't have a technical background. How can I possibly learn the skills you cited? What I call technical skills are actually analytical skills (such as data modeling) and modeling notations (such as UML). All these are things someone without a technical background can learn. You might object further—but I just don't find that technical stuff interesting. My background is more financial. To which I answer—you might want to consider a career as a PM.

Business analysis is of course not a new discipline—systems analysts have been around for as long as there have been IT systems—but its quest to professionalize itself as a discipline is recent. In its quest to professionalize itself, there has been a desire to emphasize that BAs can do much more than just systems analysis. Business analysis, the argument goes, should not limit itself to IT systems or projects. The role of business analysts, the argument continues, is to introduce and manage change within organizations, regardless of whether the change occurs within the context of a project, and regardless of whether the change involves an IT system.

This is true, and BAs who wish to learn best practices and advance their careers should hone their enterprise analysis skills, in addition to softer skills such as facilitation. The problem is that BAs are not the only ones to claim expertise in change management; everyone from management consultants to PMs to change management professionals is doing exactly that.

I argue for a different strategy: to differentiate yourself from other members of your project team, and even from other BAs, you should focus on in-demand technical skills. Enterprise analysis and change management are great, but there's nothing wrong with old-fashioned systems analysis.

Maria Amuchastegui, CBAP, CSM

Business Analysis Book of Mentors

Instructor, Business Analysis Certificate Program
Faculty of Continuing and Professional Studies
Sheridan College
E-mail: maria.amuchastegui@sheridancollege.ca
Website: www.amuchastegui.com

 Maria Amuchastegui is a Toronto-based IT consultant, educator, and writer. Her IT consulting practice combines business analysis with business architecture for clients in the government, telecommunications, healthcare, and financial sectors. She is active in the business analysis community and a contributing writer to Version 3 of the *BABOK* (*IIBA Business Analysis Body of Knowledge*). She is an instructor in the business analysis certificate program at Sheridan College.

11

Achieving Clarity of Thought

John Barris

"A kilo of noise?" The butcher roared with laughter as he heard my mother's attempt to ask for meat in broken Spanish. She had just arrived in Uruguay, and she was attempting to buy a cut of meat called *rueda*, when the butcher heard *ruido* (the Spanish word for "noise"). Since I grew up in a country foreign to my New Zealand parents, I quickly learned the need to communicate and listen with clarity.

These lessons provided me with valuable grounding for my career as a business analyst. Having a clear understanding of the business, its issues, and its requirements; and purposefully communicating with equal clarity to stakeholders the information required to either make decisions or build a system are paramount to the success of any business analyst.

In my current role of Business Change Practice Director at Equinox IT, I often explain business analysis as having "three pillars":

1. Elicitation—the ability to gather the information required to understand the topic in question
2. Analysis—making sense out of the information gathered
3. Communication—the ability to convey a message relevant to the audience (in this case, the analyzed information) to make a decision or take some action.

Clarity of thought is a key to ensuring that value is delivered through these three pillars.

Five key areas contribute to clarity of thought:
1. A clear context within which business requirements are described
2. A clear definition of what is changing and what isn't
3. A clear picture of the proposed configuration of the business capabilities required
4. A consensus on the success criteria of a project
5. An ability to work collaboratively with people

Bringing the above ingredients effectively together provides a clear understanding to decision makers of the change a business requires and to IT professionals of the specifications for systems built.

A Clear Context

Just as the context can alter a word's meaning, the context within which a business operates influences the definition and handling of its requirements. This is illustrated vividly in the story of "The Blind Men and the Elephant" in which six blind men are asked to describe an elephant. Each gives a different description based on what he can feel. So, for one, an elephant was like a snake; for the others, a tall tree, a great wall, a spear, a fan, or a rope. None could appreciate the full picture as his conclusion depended on what body part he touched.

Business architecture is a developing discipline that allows enterprise business analysts to provide executives with a suitable context to understand their business. It enables them to describe and understand the impact that significant changes might have on the business. Key to the success of business architecture is ensuring the following principles are followed:

- Keep it simple.
- Focus on breadth rather than depth.
- Know when to stop (in other words, once the purpose of the communication has been achieved).

A Clear Definition

With this in mind, I found it important to use simple terms to define the "descriptors" used for a business. For example, I use frameworks such as the Object Management Group's "Business Motivation Model" or Equinox IT's "Enterprise Analysis Framework" (see Figure 6), which has components such as Primary Activities, Business Domains, and Business Capabilities to analyze a business. However, when communicating, I use simple and intuitive language. So, when talking to business stakeholders, we call a Primary Activity "what a business does" and a Business Capability "what they need to do, what they do." Once we apply the frameworks and undertake our analysis, the results are communicated using pictures rather than a standard notation (unless this is meaningful to the business).

With a colleague, I applied this approach at Archives New Zealand by visually representing a major program of work. The resulting picture showed what Archives New Zealand would look like once the program was completed. The value of this simple and yet meaningful picture brought to stakeholders was validated by one executive's comment, "It lowered the barrier of participation."

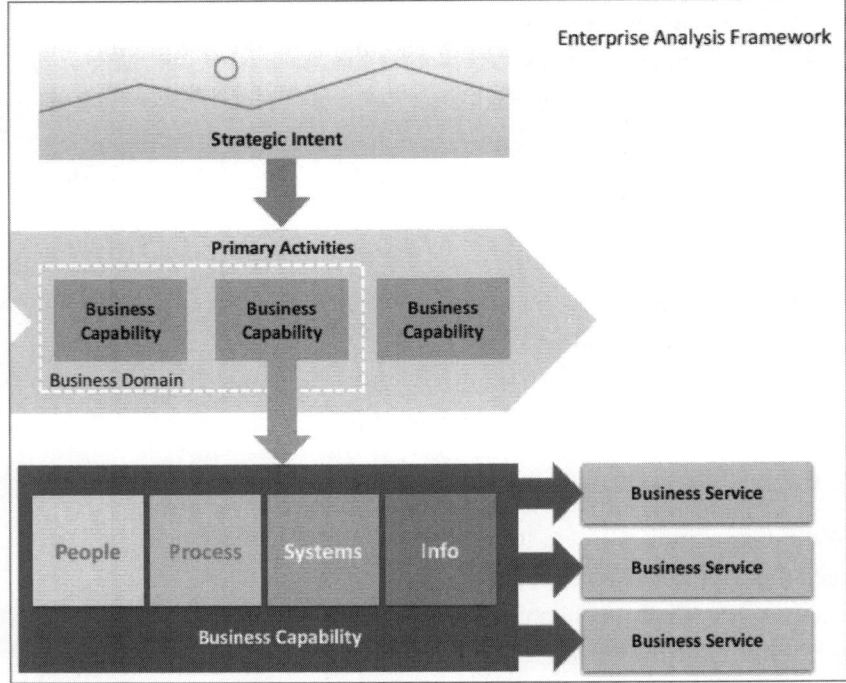

Enterprise Analysis Framework

Fig. 6. Equinox IT Enterprise Analysis Framework (used with permission from Equinox Limited)

A Clear Picture

A clear picture can portray a clear scope, leading to a clear understanding of the context of a particular business change and promoting valued discussions among stakeholders. This is possible because there is a common view. So what's changing... and what isn't?

When making renovations, builders and architects examine the existing plans of a house to determine what can be reused or adjusted and what needs to be added. In my experience, projects often fall into the trap of taking on "a life of their own." As a result, they start to redefine aspects of the business that do not need to be reevaluated. In the case of many home alterations, a new plan of the entire house is not required; the alterations simply need to be described and positioned correctly.

When businesses choose to manage their business know-how and technology as assets, I have found the ability to deliver projects is accelerated and enhanced. So, if business rules, for example, are managed as an asset in their own right, projects will not need to redefine the rules every time they seek to automate a particular business function. If data or business concepts are clearly defined and understood in the business, project glossaries would simply refer to the terms within the scope of a project rather than creating a new one (my architect colleagues call this *reuse*). If this principle is consistently applied across a wide range of business assets such as process, data, and rules, the job of defining requirements is simplified. The focus shifts to the handling of functions and the corresponding configuration of data, rules, and processes to support their automation.

These lessons became obvious when I heard of a government department that had decided to set up a "Business Rules Practice" to manage business rules. They set out to map the legislation governing the department and manage all the derived business rules and policies. As a result of the investment, changes including business rules could be deployed in a matter of days rather than months.

In short, knowing your business well and managing that knowledge can minimize the effort required to achieve a change in business needs. By minimizing the discovery aspect of the analysis effort, a business analyst can focus on the change itself, knowing that most of the data and rules are already defined. This focus provides clarity on what needs to be changed.

1. Configuration

Many people have to take many pills to deal with different ailments, and then have to take a whole set of other pills to combat the side effects of the first set. Systems also suffer from overlapping remedies. One major problem in organizations is the inability to exit legacy systems. Projects based on business cases that define the replacement of a system as one of their benefits often finish before the legacy system is replaced. As a result, many systems overlap in functionality, and workarounds are required to cover the gaps. One New Zealand bank had several core systems that needed to interact with one another to perform basic account management functions. It found itself in this situation because none of the attempts to replace a system were completed, leaving an ever-increasing collection of legacy systems.

When a system's context is defined using business language (for business capabilities and business policies), and the resources that contribute to these capabilities are managed as assets, defining solution requirements becomes more of a configuration exercise. Rather than defining the traditional "the system shall," requirements can be described as "the business requires" the ability to perform a function or provide a business service. The change, then, is defined in the following terms:

- What process needs to be adapted
- What roles need to change
- Which functions require automation or system enablement
- What information needs to be used or produced
- What policies need to be created, adjusted, or implemented

When requirements are defined as "the rearrangement, acquisition, or release of business capability," the change becomes a complete business proposition rather than a technical implementation not necessarily well understood. This approach achieves clarity of understanding of the change proposed and its impact.

2. Consensus on Success Criteria

A biblical proverb says, "Where there is no vision, the people perish." Any project that does not have a clearly articulated reason for being should be questioned. The key areas contributing to clarity of thought cited above provide the basis for defining the success criteria for a program of work. A clear understanding of what is changing, articulated in clear business terms, provides a project with a clear goal (which is to effect the change described). Achieving and maintaining consensus on the success criteria of a project is a key to maintaining the motivation and momentum of any program of work.

In one organization I worked at, the pressure to cut costs because of a lack of timely delivery drove senior management to de-scope a large program of work to the extent that it also removed many benefits on which it was based. They seemed to have forgotten the project's success criteria.

One of the most successful large-scale programs of work in which I was a stakeholder was the core systems replacement at a major bank. It was used to change how the bank viewed its customers. The executives saw that the project provided an opportunity to move the bank from an "account-centric" view to a "customer-centric" view. By training their staff with this emphasis in mind, the focus shifted from implementing a new system to introducing a new way to treat customers. This focus paid off; turning a technical implementation into a cultural change not only made the program a success, but also contributed to the bank's being ranked top in customer service. An agreed success criteria removes ambiguity and provides a clear target for a project, thus increasing its ability to succeed.

Principles of Successful Collaboration

The four key areas I have covered so far rely heavily on this last area. This is the "make or break" of any project or initiative. When it comes to systems, it is all about people, and when it comes to projects, no one can work alone! Many organizations and industries have placed significant emphasis on development methodologies. Agile and Lean approaches to software development have become popular and the topic of many conferences. My experience with Agile has not been formal. I have applied the principles of "people over processes" and "functionality over documentation" with varying degrees of success. I have learned two basic principles of successful collaboration:

1. Meaningful engagement
2. Whom you work with is more important than how you work

Sometime back, I sat in a meeting of frustrated software architects and program managers from a major program of work. The architects' complaint was that after sitting in weeks of self-imposed "reading the requirements" sessions, they felt they were no further ahead in understanding them. I got the job to sort this engagement nightmare. I facilitated a workshop with many involved parties. The solution we designed was simple and worked well when applied. The proposal was to place two different roles in a room with a common goal. In this case, business analysts and architects were to meet with the following goals and principles in mind:

- The workshop would look forward, not back.
- It would have one goal (in this case, the production of an architectural deliverable).
- Each role had different responsibilities (architects to produce the artefact, business analysts to ensure the requirements were complete and understood).
- If the requirements needed work, action would be taken outside the workshop.

Having different responsibilities contributing to the same goal became, for me, a basic principle for successful engagement. I also learned that whom you work with is more important than the approach taken. Having applied the same Agile methods within the same environment with two different people, the results were so different.

The key success factors were:

- Skilled people
- Trust and openness
- Respect for each other's skills
- Focus on the outcome rather than approach
- Very few boundaries
- Production of documentation last and/or only when you need to

Good engagement and building delivery teams with people who collaborate well contributes to a clear focus on getting the job done. Ask clearly; think clearly; speak clearly!

The above lessons have taught me that the recipe of successful business analysis is to be clear about
- Where you are working (the context)
- What you are working on (what's changing)
- What's available and how to use it (configuration)
- What's good enough (success criteria)
- Whom you are working with (collaboration)

My mother quickly learned the value of clarity when shopping for meat. The ability to learn these lessons has helped me help others see clearly what they need to do.

John Barris
Equinox Limited
Level 12, Equinox House, 111 The Terrace, PO Box 10 168,
Wellington 6143 New Zealand
T +64.4.499.9450
E-mail: john.barris@equinox.co.nz
Website: www.equinox.co.nz
LinkedIn: John Barris

John is a kiwi born in Uruguay, South America. He has a banking background. He has worked as a business analyst at several levels of organizations and managed business analysis teams. He is currently the Business Change Practice Director at Equinox Ltd, a New Zealand consulting and software development company that also provides training services.

Business Analysis Book of Mentors

John is a practicing member of the International Institute of Business Analysts (IIBA) and an associate member of the Financial Services Institute of Australasia (Finsia). He is also one of the first kiwis to become a Certified Business Analysis Professional (CBAP).

With nearly 20 years of experience in business analysis, John is sought for his ability to assess and clearly scope and define opportunities for business improvement and change. His analysis, coaching, and leadership experience equips him to provide a range of business analysis, enterprise analysis, and business change consulting, training, and mentoring services. He also speaks at industry events and as a guest lecturer at Victoria University, Wellington, New Zealand.

Seeing the Big Picture

"The trick to forgetting the big picture is to look at everything close-up." - Chuck Palahniuk

12

Solve the Right Problem by Understanding the Big Picture

Kathleen Barret

The capacity to understand and act on the big picture is the single most important competency or skill you will need as a business analyst (BA) needs to develop professionally. This analytical ability is the first step in effective organizational change; it provides the context needed to evaluate potential options and solutions. Without the big picture, organizations can only make the right choices accidentally.

As the business analyst, your role is partly conceptual artist depicting the organizational possibilities. An organization is composed of operational and change systems. Operational systems represent the factory or production side of the business that generates value for its stakeholders. Change systems alter operational systems to make them more efficient or effective. Business analysis is a change system—the practice of enabling change in an organizational context by defining needs and recommending solutions that deliver value to stakeholders. Because many change initiatives happen concurrently in an organization, a BA who understands the big picture can help others understand how all the potential changes fit together.

Organizations are under constant external pressure—increased competition, smarter customers, growing government regulation, and a turbulent economic climate. Management often makes decisions based on a short-time horizon—reacting to, instead of planning for or anticipating, changes. By understanding the big picture, and helping others understand the context in which changes happen, BAs can help their organizations focus on the most important activities and respond and adapt to change, instead of just reacting to change.

Only by working with co-creators can you access all the details of the big picture. The BA works with many stakeholders to help them clarify needs to address gaps and respond to opportunities. The constraints of time and money and potentially conflicting requirements require stakeholders to choose what is most critical. Understanding the big picture *provides a context* in which to assess the different solution options.

Understanding the big picture is often a significant gap overlooked in a project team, including by the project sponsor and business lead. Individually, we focus on execution, getting stuff done, instead of understanding what needs doing. Organizations can discourage understanding the big picture by rewarding quick execution without thought of purpose, penalizing individuals who step outside the well-defined boundaries of project roles and responsibilities. In your role as BA, you can help facilitate understanding of the big picture within teams, including that of managers and executives, and help ensure the right changes are made.

The Industry Standard

IIBA best practices for defining the big picture are shared in the Enterprise Analysis knowledge area of *The Guide to the Business Analysis Body of Knowledge (BABOK® Guide)*—What is the goal of the change initiative? What are some solution options? What is the culture of the organization? What are measures of success? Without clear goals and direction, the most efficiently executed project can deliver the wrong solution.

The Enterprise Analysis category in the IIBA Business Analysis Competency Model contains 10 discipline competencies, all which are important to understanding the big picture. Of these, the most important is "Identify and define business need," which includes five behaviors.

- *Why change?* What is missing from the current system, process, or business capability? What is the gap between where the organization is now and where it has to be to remain successful? Answering this question requires a big picture perspective on what the organization is trying to achieve.

- *Understand needs.* Senior leadership often focuses on tactical business needs—what problems do I have to solve today? Understanding the big picture keeps your sights on the strategic needs of the organization so you can ensure it will be around tomorrow.

- *Align needs to goals.* The foundation of the big picture is the organization's vision and goals. Does addressing the identified gap support the goals of the organization? If it doesn't, you might be trying to solve the wrong problem or one that will not support the organizational direction.

- *Define objectives.* The gap between the current and future state can be dealt with through several solutions. Understanding the components of the different options and their support of the big picture allows you to assess and prioritize them to deliver the greatest value.

- *Capture the real vision.* Vision statements can often be vague, open-ended, or point to a solution. Referencing the big picture in discussions with stakeholders provides a context in which to assess and provide clarity around the vision statements.

Systems Thinking

Another term that captures the idea of the big picture is systems thinking. Although not truly the opposite, systems thinking is often considered to contrast with analytical thinking. Here, it gets tricky for a business analysis professional. By definition, a BA is "analytical," naturally decomposing problems into pieces to understand where there is a gap or opportunity. Systems thinking, on the other hand, focuses on the relationship between the parts—how they work together over time and within the context of a larger system, and how the elements of a system feed back to one another. Effective business analysis requires the business analyst see not just the whole, but also the relationship among the pieces. To use a common metaphor—the BA needs to *see the forest and the trees.*

System: A group of interacting, interrelated, interdependent, and heterogeneous components that form a complex and unified whole. The system maintains its existence and functions as a whole through the interaction of its parts.

A Real-Life Example

I was asked by a senior BA in the Corporate Services area of a large Canadian bank to assist in identifying high-level business requirements for an ad hoc reporting system. This solution would be used to query a data warehouse containing all the financial data for the bank captured monthly. The reporting system would support all the lines of business of the Bank (commercial, retail, wholesale, and so on) and was sponsored by the chief accountants from each division, five senior executives. In my role as the Manager of the Business Analysis Centre of Competency (BA CoC), I looked at ways to educate senior leadership on the benefits of business analysis.

There was much sensitivity around this project. The Bank had already spent close to $200 million on the financial database, but access to the data was limited to standardized reports. An ad hoc query capability could help justify the investment by making all the information available as needed without having to engage the information technology department. A successful project would increase support and provide great advertising for the system.

Developing the Operational Vision (OV)

The senior BA and I decided the best approach was to bring the various accounting executives from each business line together in a workshop to define what a successful future state would be. We used a technique called an Operational Vision to help identify the business and, more specifically, project objectives. An Operational Vision (OV), often called *guiding principles*, is a document that describes how the client wants to operate in the future. It directly relates to the processes found in that client world and describes principles those processes should follow if they are to align with a future vision.

An OV facilitates the identification of project objectives by capturing and defining the future state and then determining what has to be in place to satisfy and deliver the future state. These implication statements expose the gaps which might exist between the existing world and the future state and represent the high-level changes that must occur to achieve the vision. Once captured, the implications are sorted based on priority, impact, timeline or phase, ease of implementation, and owner. Project objectives and scope are drawn from the prioritized implication statements, and they generally represent only a subset of the total.

The advantages of having an OV are:
- Creates a common understanding of direction
- Facilitates decision making and minimizes misunderstandings, misinterpretations, and confusion about the direction

At the workshop, once the meeting objectives and introductions had been made, I described a future state scenario. In three years' time, the Bank would be publicly recognized for its ability to respond and quickly adapt to the changing business environment. Participants were asked to describe what had happened to enable this change to occur. These ideas were captured on separate flipcharts throughout the room—one sheet of paper for each idea.

Below are examples of the OV statements developed during the workshop:

1. The Bank makes information available to whomever needs it in an accessible and usable form.
2. The Bank manages and controls access to information.
3. The Bank leverages its data to make better decisions to manage the business and maximize enterprise profitability.
4. The Bank makes decisions based on complete and accurate data.

Visions and Implications

Once agreed to by the group, these statements became the OV or business goals. The group then discussed each vision statement and brainstormed what activities needed to happen to achieve these outcomes. They were captured as implication statements. One-by-one, we walked through each vision statement and its associated implications. Here, the value of the OV technique was realized. Most of us are guilty of thinking our perspectives are understood and people agree with us. The implication statements uncovered conflicts and other misalignments across the business units. The first phase of solution scoping began with the elimination of these conflicting needs.

The second scoping phase happened after reviewing each item, prioritizing them, assessing the technical and business complexity associated with each, and identifying linkages or dependencies. By sorting by the highest-level priority, less important objectives could be discounted or eliminated.

The team continued to meet over the next few weeks to review the evolving OV statements and implications and assess the impacts of the different potential solutions. The group realized that any solution at this time would deliver a less-than-sufficient solution. Based on the input from the Accounting executives, the Bank decided to cancel the project. By staying focused on the big picture in our discussions, we ensured a clear understanding of the project's expectations. The multiple project sponsors could clearly assess the long-term benefits against the risk and expense. The senior BA and I demonstrated an often overlooked and underappreciated benefit of business analysis— preventing a project from happening.

Although I used this technique for an enterprise project, it can be just as easily applied to smaller projects. One of my peers uses it for even minor changes to current applications. The benefit of this approach is multifold. The group environment allows for the cross-pollination of ideas and helps stakeholders formulate and formalize their requirements. Perspectives are shared, differences identified and discussed and, hopefully, resolved. The project team will get a clear understanding of goals and objectives, and the stakeholders will have confidence that the solution will deliver value. The biggest challenge will be determining who the decision makers are and getting their commitment to participate.

Critical Success Factors

Like any technique, the approach I took to drive consensus among high-powered stakeholders required support from my leadership team as well as a clearly defined plan. Below are other critical success factors.

- Make sure you have the appropriate sponsorship (firepower) to get the right people in the room. In an IT project, this might be a business sponsor, a project sponsor, or a project manager.

- Make sure stakeholders understand why you are doing what you are doing. Don't assume they understand the value of business analysis. To them, it is probably a waste of time. Don't say, "This is a process." Your process is their red tape.

- Be clear about expectations of meetings—purpose and outcome—and stick to your schedule. People respect you when you respect their time.
- Be prepared. You destroy credibility through sloppiness.
- Be neutral. Capture and synthesize input but avoid emotion-packed words. Restate understanding and ask for agreement and consensus. If business analysis were a color, it would be beige.

- Use the simplest tool possible and make sure everyone understands the approach, output, and use.

- Manage the discussion, but let it flow if it helps resolve confusion or clarify positions (a fine balance—the art of business analysis).

- Keep referring to the big picture when discussions go off topic. It is the cornerstone of your change initiative!

Getting the Big Picture

Most of us are guilty of thinking that others have a similar understanding of the big picture. Defining a context, articulating the future state, and getting a formal agreement with your stakeholders on what the big picture is ensures you deal with the highest priority problem or opportunity

.

Make sure you understand the *correct* big picture.

The big picture is made up of several components. Externally, it includes the competition, customer, government, and global economy. Internally, it includes information technology, organizational history, current structure, and internal politics. By understanding the context in which the change occurs and performing a comprehensive stakeholder analysis, a BA can most accurately define the big picture. To reuse the previous metaphor with a slight twist—*you have to see the trees within the forest*. Here is an example in which I saw the forest but missed some critical trees.

In my role as Manager of the Business Analysis Centre of Competency, I was asked to revise the career ladder for the business analysis role and lead a project to formalize who performs what activities throughout the project lifecycle. Often, project teams spent quite a bit of time upfront determining roles and responsibilities. Defining a high-level RACI chart (Responsible, Accountable, Consult, and Inform) could have potentially improved project efficiency. The exercise was not to be exhaustive, but instead to focus on the key deliverables and roles in Information Technology. The project sponsor was the vice president in charge of application development.

To me, the goal was obvious—identify critical IT deliverables and determine who was accountable for delivering them. The solution would not be based on "what is" but "what should be," according to the role descriptions. The big picture—make the applications group more efficient and provide staff with a clear understanding of expectations about their performance. Unfortunately, I failed to recognize all the components that make up the context of the big picture, particularly the politics and history.

The sponsoring VP had been successful because of his relationships with his leadership team. Although he wanted to improve the efficiency of his operations, he knew he couldn't change too much too quickly as he would alter the power structure. Nothing would happen if his team decided not to comply. The second miss was my lack of appreciation of the power of complacency. People might not be happy in their current roles, but that doesn't mean they want to change. Complacency is comfortable. If the individuals who would be affected didn't embrace the change, it would not happen.

The big picture can be different depending on who you are and where you sit in the organization. Besides looking at the objective factors, you also need to understand the motives of key decision makers. What do they expect to gain from the change? What will they lose? A thorough impact analysis will uncover not just the potential outcomes of the change, but also the side effects. For many stakeholders, those indirect outcomes are the true motivation behind the project.

The obvious big picture might not be the accurate one. Make sure you understand all dimensions of the context before proceeding.

The One Piece of Advice

Before you proceed with any change initiative, understand the big picture affecting the need for the change. Focus on both external and internal influences. Involve your co-creators by ensuring you engage the appropriate stakeholders and understand the underlying motivation of key decision makers. Together, define the future state and have a shared, clear vision of where the organization needs to be to continue to be successful.

Use this new understanding to help facilitate the prioritization of needs and eliminate less important requirements. Help your stakeholders understand the necessary trade-offs to deliver the greatest value to the organization.

Big Picture Questions

The following questions will guide you in the creation of the big picture.
What is happening externally?

- Who are your competitors? What are their products?
- Who is your customer? Why do they buy from you?
- Are there new government regulations and requirements?
- How is the economy performing?

What is the internal context?
- What are the vision and goals of the organization?
- What is its current capability? How big is the gap?
- Who are key influencers? What is the true motivation behind the change?
- What does success look like?

Kathleen Barret
T 416-417-6327
Twitter: @kathleenbarret
Website:kthleenbarret.com

Kathleen is a recognized leader and visionary in business analysis. She founded and led the professional association for business analysts (International Institute of Business Analysis (IIBA®)) since its inception in 2003 to August 2013.

Under Kathleen's direction, IIBA grew from a completely volunteer-based organization with 37 members to a global organization with 29 staff and more than 26,000 members in 120-plus countries and more than $5 million in revenue. As a virtual company, IIBA presented unique challenges. With her staff, Kathleen developed tools and approaches to support this nontraditional environment, and she is currently writing a book about how to create, run, and sustain a virtual organization.

Throughout her career, Kathleen's focus has been to improve organization performance either as an external consultant or in a staff role. From IT benchmarking to health checks, her approach has incorporated the four pillars or organizational capabilities: process, tools, information, and people. However, Kathleen believes that people provide the competitive advantage in the market. Everyone can do technology, have great processes, but it is organizations that know how to leverage their most valuable and unique resource—their people— that will survive and thrive in business.

Kathleen is a noted keynote speaker and instructor and has presented at conferences all over the world on:

- The evolution and future of business analysis
- Developing your staff and organizational capability
- Creating and sustaining virtual organizations

13

Focus on What Makes Your Business Smart: Business Rules

Gladys Lam

When a business builds or revises a business capability, on what do your business stakeholders concentrate? Four very natural areas are:

1. People—We need good people. Human Resources departments have been around for a long time. They are set up to help manage people.
2. Technologies—Technologies have been around since the

invention of machines. Organizations are familiar with dealing with technology changes.

3. Information—Information was a big deal in the 1980s and 1990s during the information management era. Big data is now a hot topic in many organizations.

4. Process—Business process management and business process re-engineering have been popular since the 1990s. Many techniques offered in this area.

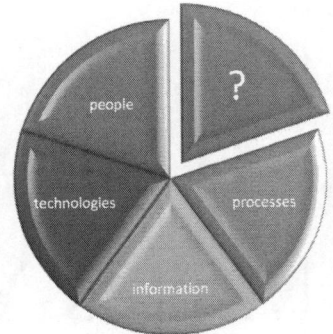

Now, what is missing? What is the fifth piece that completes the pie? For your business capability to produce maximum benefit, it needs to be SMART. So what makes a business capability smart?

A process might be efficient, but the guidance to avoid mistakes and make intelligent judgments makes a capability smart.

Information might be collected and managed, but the use of the information to make proper decisions makes a capability smart.

Technology might be state-of-the-art, but the application of the technologies to guide behavior and operations makes a capability smart.

People might work at maximum capacity, but their intellect makes a capability smart.

A business capability is smart when it uses people, technologies, information, and processes to make the right decisions and

Five components make your business smart:

1. Operational strategies
2. Business concepts
3. Business rules
4. Operational business decisions
5. Key performance indicators
6.

Collectively, we refer to these elements as the Operational IP (intellectual property) of your business.

Organizations are in various stages of managing their Operational IP. In this chapter, I explore one of the most talked about components in Operational IP—business rules.

What Is a Business Rule?

One of the best parts of my job is the opportunity to visit major organizations worldwide. In guiding organizations in adapting a business rules approach, one of the first things that becomes clearly apparent is different people perceive business rules differently. So, if you embark on a project focusing on business rules, do not assume everyone knows what a business rule is or assume everyone thinks about business rules the way you do.

Some people might think business rules are requirements: "Provide a feature to handle electronic funds transfer." Some people might think business rules are use-case statements: "Customer provides account ID. System displays account information." Some people might think business rules are system *if/then* statements: "If the overdrawn flag is set to 'yes,' then reject transaction."

What is a business rule? The definition I like is:
A business rule is a criterion used in business operations to

- Guide behavior
- Shape judgments
- Make decisions[1]

By that definition, business rules related to the requirement, use case, and system if/then statement given above might be, respectively:

"Each employee expense reimbursement must be processed through electronic funds transfer."

"A customer must have a valid account ID."

"An account must not be overdrawn." "An account may be considered overdrawn only if the amount of a cash withdrawal is greater than the balance of the account at the time of the withdrawal."

A business rules approach makes you ask the business questions first. Notice how the business rule statements above are about the business, not the system. Your business needs these business rules, even if there are no automated systems.

Remember that business rules guide your business operation. A business rule tells you what you may or may not do in a business environment.

What Is the Big Deal?

Haven't we been implementing business rules since the beginning of time? Yes, of course! We have always implemented rules. You need the right payroll calculation rules to calculate the right payroll amounts. You need the right distribution rules to ensure the right inventory is sent out of the right warehouse.

So what is the big deal? The big deal is that with the advent of the technology and internet age, there is a need to make change faster—

---

[1] Ronald G. Ross with Gladys S.W. Lam, Building Business Solutions: Business Analysis with Business Rules, An IIBA® Sponsored Handbook, Business Rule Solutions, LLC, October 2011, http://www.brsolutions.com/bbs.

especially critical is the need to change business rules quickly to keep up with business needs. The problems with the traditional ways are that:

- Business rules are imbedded in systems
- Business people don't know their business rules
- Business people have no control of their business rules
- Business people cannot manage their Operational IP (that is, business rules)

If your business needs to change a business rule, it can no longer afford to wait six months, three months, or even one week for IT to make a change. To stay competitive and provide customer service in this rapidly developing information age, it is imperative that businesses:

- Know their business rules
- Assess impact
- Make changes quickly

Given the continuous evolution of business needs and the IT industry, business rules management has to be the next big thing. Just think—once a business has omnipotent power with its data, what would it want next? Data is dormant. It is after the fact. You can build enormous data warehouses to analyze your data. You will know your customer trends, your product sales, and your employee behaviors, but what good is knowing if you can't act on it? How do you act on it? Business rules! Remember, business rules tell your business what you may or may not do. You change and enforce behavior and decisions through business rules.

Business rules help make your business smart!

Consider this example:

You discover from your data that the slowest period in your retail store is 8:00 a.m. to 9:00 a.m. You figure you have two options to increase profitability:

1. To generate business during those hours, you could introduce an early-bird morning sale—20% off all items in the store between 8:00 a.m. and 9:00 a.m.
2. To save costs, you could change the opening hours to 9:00 a.m.

Your business simply cannot afford to wait a long time for these changes. You want to introduce discounts or reschedule workers in a real time manner. What if this store is part of a chain of stores? How quickly can you act? How quickly can you analyze the impact of this change?

A business rules approach gives the business the capability to identify, analyze, implement, and manage the change in a timely and efficient manner.

Where Is the Challenge?

Business rules are rules about the business. Therefore, it shouldn't take a rocket scientist to tell you that business rules should come from the business (that is, business people should specify the business rules, not IT).

Traditionally, IT gathers rules from the business. The team then goes away, hides for months on end, and finally, converts those rules to a language that takes a university degree to understand. The business is too intimidated to challenge those rules or the brains that created them. IT is thought of as mystical. Any rule change requires a formal invitation for the wizards to come out and do their magic. (Then, you pray it will work.)

This doesn't fly anymore in today's environment. Desktop and mobile computing enable business people to be their own wizards. You should see the complexity in some Excel spreadsheets I have reviewed. Business people want more control. A business rule-focused approach allows that.

Now, back to what is so difficult about business rules. Business rules are difficult to find—that's what. Every business we go to has business rules—hundreds and thousands of rules. Where are they? In people's heads, in existing codes built by the wizards of yesteryears, in policy manuals, in outdated user guides, and so on. What is difficult is specifying the right business rules for the right situations.

What Is the Solution?

The easy answer is to buy some better software. I have seen too many organizations fall into the trap of buying software in the hopes of solving their problems. Millions of dollars are spent on technology skills to learn how to use the software. What is always forgotten is how the business side fits in.

To build a smart business capability, you need a solid approach to gather, analyze, and manage business rules. What people always forget is that the key to success is in the consideration of what to put in a tool, not simply the tool itself. Giving MS Word to someone does not magically enable the person to write. You get all the bells and whistles with the tool, but without the right content, it is still useless.

Embarking on a business rules approach is no different. Simply acquiring a powerful rules or decision engine does not guarantee success. There are many wonderful business rules and decision-management tools in the market today; don't get me wrong. The tool is important. I am saying that the technology is there. However, the real benefit to a business rules approach is its ability to connect the business directly to its business rules.

The key is knowing how to gather and manage business rules from the business and how to connect them to technology implementations. Here, business analysts can make a significant difference. Business analysts play a major role in

- Capturing business rules from
  - Subject-area experts in facilitated sessions or one-on-one interviews
  - Documentation by identifying processes, decisions, and policies and by asking the right questions to extract business rules
  - System code by reversing engineering system logic to business logic, and distinguishing business rules from system rules

- Specifying business rules by
  - Writing business rule statements consistently
  - Developing decision structure
  - Creating decision tables

- Analyzing business rules for
  - Duplication, redundancy, subsumptions, and conflicts
  - Impact on existing rules when a rule is changed, deleted, or added
  - Reuse of existing business rules instead of creating new ones for each initiative or each business area

- Managing business rules to
  - Provide governance when business rule changes are needed
  - Organize a large set of business rules
  - Report on business rules from different perspectives
  - Establish the relationship among business rules or business rule sets
  - Set up the traceability of business rules from source to implementation

What Is Next?

I concentrated mostly on business rules in this chapter. Business rules are often the entry point to all the other areas in your Operational IP.

Another significant area in Operational IP is operational decisions. I encourage business analysts to take advantage of our free white papers on that topic. You can also find out more about Operational IP from our blogs, articles, books, training, and conferences.
Remember...

- Your business Operational IP (intellectual property) makes your business smart!
- Business rules are a central component of your Operational IP.
- Your Operational IP puts the power back to the business to drive the business solution.

To complete the pie graph in the beginning of the chapter, remember that your Operational IP represents the intellect of your business. Focus on what makes your business smart.

Together these elements build a smart business capability.

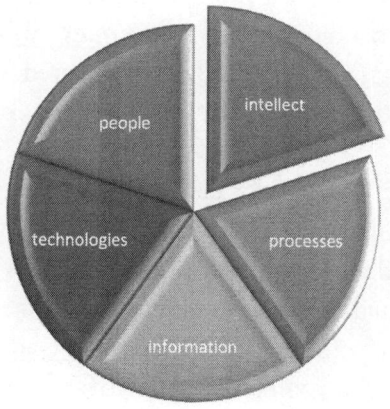

Business Analysis Book of Mentors

Gladys Lam
E-mail: glam@BRSolutions.com
Twitter: @GladysLam

Gladys S. W. Lam is a world-renowned authority on applied business rule and decision techniques. She is principal and cofounder of Business Rule Solutions, LLC (www.BRSolutions.com), the most recognized company worldwide in business rules and decision analysis. Ms. Lam is co-creator of IPSpeak™, the BRS methodology. She is cofounder of *BRCommunity.com*, a vertical community for professionals and home of *Business Rules Journal*. She coauthored *Building Business Solutions: Business Analysis With Business Rules*, an IIBA®-sponsored handbook on business analysis with business rules, with Ronald G. Ross.

Ms. Lam is widely known for her lively, pragmatic style. She is an internationally recognized expert on business rules and decision techniques. She speaks internationally at conferences and other professional events and co-presents interactive online seminars. She is also executive director of the Building Business Capability (BBC) Conference—the official conference of the IIBA®—which includes the Business Rules Forum, .

Ms. Lam is a world-renowned expert on business project management, who has managed many projects focusing on the large-scale capture, analysis, and management of business rules and decisions. She works comfortably with senior executives, providing insights and advice. She advises senior management of large companies on organizational issues and on business solutions to business problems. She is most effective in mentoring and training business analysts worldwide.

Ms. Lam is most recognized for her ability to identify the source of business issues and effectiveness in developing pragmatic approaches to resolve them. She has gained an excellent reputation for fostering positive professional relationships with principals and support staff in projects.

Contact Gladys directly, <u>Glam@BRSolutions.com,</u> to learn more about the method and techniques described in this chapter.

About Business Rule Solutions

Business Rule Solutions, LLC is the recognized world leader in the advancement of business rules and decision management. Cofounders Ronald G. Ross and Gladys S. W. Lam are internationally acclaimed as the foremost experts and practitioners of related techniques and methodology.

Since its inception in 1996, BRS has helped pilot the worldwide growth of business rules. BRS offers IPSpeak^{TM}, its groundbreaking methodology for business rules, decision logic, and business vocabulary (concept models), including the popular RuleSpeak®, DecisionSpeak^{TM}, TableSpeak^{TM}, and ConceptSpeak^{TM}. BRS services include consulting, online interactive training, in-house workshops, publications, and presentations. For more information about BRS, visit <u>www.BRSolutions.com</u>.

14

Design Thinking: Taking Business Analysis to the Next Level

Jay Payette

The business analysis profession has gone through considerable evolution and maturation over the past 10 years. At the turn of the century, the business analyst's role was difficult to define. Many organizations had different interpretations of what a business analyst's responsibilities were and what activities could be called business analysis. That all changed when the IIBA® was formed in Toronto in

2003. Trouble was, some analysts mistook *standards* for the *gold standard* of business analysis, which led to complacency.

What Does a Business Analyst Do?

"What exactly does a business analyst do anyway?" can now be answered. One of the IIBA's main missions was to create a formal definition of business analysis by establishing common standards, processes, a taxonomy, artifacts, and knowledge areas. This mission was accomplished in 2008 when the version 1.6 of the *Guide to the Business Analysis Body of Knowledge®* (or simply *BABOK®*) was published in 2008. The *BABOK®* has been instrumental in helping define business analysis as a profession. It also provides a clear set of best practices for organizations, helping them define the role of the business analyst in their organization. Like most bodies of knowledge, it set the bar for what an individual should do to associate himself or herself with a certain profession, in this case, the business analysis profession.

The *BABOK®* is a wonderful thing, but both experienced and aspiring business analysts should view it as a starting point to their careers, not an endpoint. Standards establish what is *good enough*, but they don't define excellence. Adopting best practices can only allow you to catch up with the best, not surpass them. Once upon a time, having all the knowledge in the *BABOK®* made you an exceptional business analyst. However, now that the helpful folks at the IIBA® have collected all those best practices and published them conveniently in one document, the bar for the entire profession has been raised. While this was a good development for everyone, it forced experienced business analysts such as myself to step back and think about what a high-performing business analyst at the very top of the profession looked like in the new post-*BABOK®* world.

This struggle to go beyond the *BABOK®* took me in many directions. Instinctively, I turned to interpersonal skills. Being a business analyst is a very social existence. Business analysts are constantly interacting with a seemingly endless cast of personalities.

Senior managers, end users, engineers, lawyers, the public, accountants, introverts, extroverts, Type-A personalities, Type-B personalities—you name it, and I have had to interact with them. Each individual is unique, and business analysts must be prepared to communicate and empathize with any person.

Interpersonal skills are critical for any business analyst to succeed, and their salience to the profession has been well documented for some time now. Strength in such underlying competencies is widely considered to be a key differentiator between good business analysts and great business analysts. In the post-*BABOK*® world, everyone knew the importance of interpersonal skills, and everyone worked on developing them.

Forward Thinking That Creates the Market

My perspective began to change, however, when I began to look for insights outside the traditional sphere of enterprise solution creation. I became particularly fascinated with the design of consumer products such as smartphones, kitchen appliances, furniture, and even automobiles. Many leading consumer products performed the same tasks as their competitors did but did so in new and more effective ways. Companies such as Dyson seemed to understand the requirements of their end users (that is, cleaning floors, carpets, and furniture) and used innovation to develop more effective or efficient ways of meeting those requirements (that is, bagless cyclone suction).

Another breed of consumer product firms caught my attention, however. Their revolutionary products did more than meet existing requirements in a new way. These companies satisfied user requirements the consumer was not even asking to be dealt with, requirements the consumers did not even know they had.

The Blackberry product changed the world of communications by making e-mail available on a mobile device. Although the demand for a mobile e-mail device was miniscule (if existent at all) when the first Blackberry device was launched, executives around the world were soon clinging to their Blackberry devices night and day. If you asked those executives how they worked before their Blackberry, they would probably respond that they "don't know how they lived without it." Products such as the Blackberry, the Apple iPhone (the Blackberry's eventual successor), Netflix video streaming, and even the Model-T Ford changed the ways people lived and worked because they foresaw a huge demand for something for which no one explicitly asked.

Lessons From Design Thinking

Studying these iconic products and their impact on society left me wondering. If such an incredible demand can be created among a remarkably diverse population (such as North American consumers) for a solution to a problem this diverse population did not even know it had, how is it that we still screw up requirements for an enterprise IT project? Was it because these large organizations had access to incredibly expensive elicitation tools? Given Steve Jobs' famous antipathy for market research, I would say no. Did some secret technological advance enable these great projects? Again, I discovered the answer was no; after all, a technology without an application is of little use to anyone. What I did discover was that all these revolutionary products have exceptional design in common.

At this point, you might be asking yourself why any of this product design talk is important. "Design and business analysis are completely different fields using completely different skill sets," you might be saying aloud, and you would be partly correct in that statement. However, not completely correct, because some overlap exists between the two fields. Both business analysts and designers seek to develop a clear understanding of specific components of the environment around them and turn that understanding into useable output, be it a requirements document or a new toaster. In this area of discovery and understanding, business analysts can learn much from the methods, practices, and skill sets used by design professionals (collectively called *design thinking*).

Captured, Uncaptured and Undiscovered Requirements

The role design thinking plays in business analysis becomes more apparent when we look at requirements in a slightly different way. Traditionally, when business analysts classify requirements, we organize them based on their content, such as functional/nonfunctional. If, however, we want to classify requirements by the degree to which they are visible to the business analyst, we can bundle requirements into three categories: captured requirements, uncaptured requirements, and undiscovered requirements.

Captured requirements are those that have been identified by the requirement owner, elicited by the business analyst, and recorded in a document such as a requirements traceability matrix or requirements package. Another way of thinking of captured requirements is as those requirements that have entered the Requirements Management process.

Uncaptured requirements are those that have been identified by the requirement owner, but not captured by the business analyst. An example of an uncaptured requirement would be if the CEO and VP of Marketing decided their company's new website should be offered in both English and Spanish for the first time, but the website redesign project is unaware of this decision. If the website redesign project were to move forward without capturing this requirement, it would be considered a miss, and it could possibly result in a considerable change request. Uncaptured requirements only become captured requirements when they are elicited from their owners by a business analyst, and they enter the Requirements Management process.

The third type of requirement is undiscovered requirements. A stakeholder has a rough concept of these requirements, but he is unable to adequately articulate them. Let's say the VP of Marketing in our previous website redesign project example knows users have complained that the registration process is too arduous, but has little more detail. Simply stating that the new website must have a user-friendly registration process is too vague to be a useful requirement.

The VP of Marketing has a high-level concept of what her requirements are, but she has not yet discovered specifically what they are. Almost limitless combinations of requirements can satisfy the VP of Marketing's need to improve the user experience of the registration process on the website. A good business analyst will find a set of detailed requirements that satisfy her high-level requirements. A great business analyst will find that ideal set of detailed requirements which best satisfy the high-level requirements. Revealing these undiscovered requirements and finding the right combination to meet a stakeholder's true needs is where design thinking can play a crucial role for any business analyst. The design profession has taken the transformation of discovery and understanding into ideal outputs farther than any other profession has.

Going Beyond Standard Requirements

In my experience, when faced with a requirement that is too high level or vague, most business analysts will politely explain the detail they require and characteristics of a good requirement as outlined in the *BABOK®*. Although there is nothing wrong with this response, there is nothing exceptional about it, either. Business analysts are usually expected to capture uncaptured requirements. That part of the job is straightforward, and anyone with a good understanding of the *BABOK®* should do a decent job of it. Where great business analysts go beyond expectations is by explaining that a high-level requirement is too vague and then leading the requirement owners through the discovery process of understanding their true wants and needs, which leads to the detail needed in good requirements. By leading the requirements discovery process as opposed to simply collecting uncaptured requirements, business analysts can add value to their projects.

By studying the methods designers use to understand users better than the users understand themselves, business analysts can become very good at helping stakeholders discover what their requirements are. Design research methods such as ethnography, personas, mind mapping, journey mapping, visualization tools, low fidelity prototyping, reframing, minimum viable product, and co-creation have allowed me to help clients discover their real requirements much more effectively than interviews, workshops, traditional brainstorming, or affinity diagrams ever did.

That is not to say that tried-and-true elicitation techniques should be completely abandoned. They became popular for a reason, but if you want to do more than simply collect requirements that already exist in the heads of stakeholders and if you want to *lead* the identification of undiscovered requirements, I suggest that you complement your existing elicitation techniques with design thinking.

Below is a list of books I have found particularly useful in developing my design thinking skills (in no particular order):

- *Design Thinking: Integrating Innovation, Customer Experience, and Brand Value* by Thomas Lockwood
- *Universal Methods of Design: 100 Ways to Research Complex Problems, Develop Innovative Ideas, and Design Effective Solutions by Bruce Hanington and Bella Martin*
- *101 Design Methods: A Structured Approach for Driving Innovation in Your Organization by Vijay Kumar*
- *The Opposable Mind by Roger Martin*

I hope very much that you, too, can discover the power of the design thinking business analyst.

E-mail: jay@payetteconsulting.com
Twitter: @PayetteIdeas
Website: jaypayette.com
LinkedIn: /in/payette
Website: payetteconsulting.com

Jay Payette is the managing principal and founder of Payette Consulting, a boutique management consulting firm that focuses on design thinking, business analysis and design, and project management. Jay started Payette Consulting to help clients use design thinking to improve solution creation, business architecture, and the management of projects. Before founding Payette Consulting, Jay worked in the Canadian consulting practice of Accenture as a project manager and business analyst for many organizations, including Fortune 500 companies, startups, and public sector organizations across North America. Before joining Accenture, Jay worked as an independent IT consultant in the public sector.

Jay has spoken on business analysis, design thinking, and project management at many conferences, including Business Analyst World and the PMI Global Congress, and has contributed to the FIELDS interdisciplinary design journal. He currently lives in Ottawa with his wife and son.

To Innovate, to Thrive, to Plan

"When you innovate, you've got to be prepared for everyone telling you you're nuts." - Larry Ellison

15

It's All in the Plan

Jared Gorai

It's All in the Plan

Benjamin Franklin once said, "Failing to plan is planning to fail."[1][2] It's cliché, but true. As a junior business analyst, I didn't see the value of planning and left things to chance. Although, sometimes, things all fall into place, they usually don't. Things happen for a reason, and usually that reason has much to do with the planning which went into a project.

1

[2] Benjamin Franklin, BrainyQuote.com,
http://www.brainyquote.com/quotes/quotes/b/benjaminfr138217.html.

What not to do...

I remember feeling gung-ho on my first real project. I was going to use SMART requirements, my business users would all love the solution we delivered, and it would all be so easy. It didn't turn out that way. By the time I had been allocated to the project, the developers were waiting for requirements to be delivered. The project manager's Gantt chart decided that to fit into her schedule, I'd need to have my requirements completed by the following Tuesday.

Without ammunition to back me up, I set out with a gung-ho attitude. Half my stakeholders weren't available to meet me, and the other half weren't sure what we were trying to accomplish. Needless to say, without a plan, Tuesday might as well have been the following month because there was no way I would get the requirements completed by the deadline, and I didn't.

I pleaded for more time and ended up missing that deadline, too. I didn't understand that my requirements wouldn't be wrapped up with a one-hour meeting involving all my stakeholders. I hadn't accounted for time for revisions or any time to validate and approve the requirements. Ultimately, I received sign-off, but I didn't achieve the success I'd originally envisioned.

Planning 101: The Mark of the Stakeholder

All our efforts in business analysis revolve around our stakeholders. We manage their expectations, we elicit their requirements, and we deliver their solutions. If they are such key components in our lives, shouldn't our planning involve them, too?

Starting With an IGOE

I've learned over the years to start with an IGOE (Inputs, Guides, Outputs, and Enablers) chart. In it, we can better understand the components of our system and the people and processes it touches. For this chapter, I have focused my thoughts on the people involved, although an IGOE chart contains much more than just the stakeholders. Filling this chart out doesn't take long, but it ensures I've at least accounted for all stakeholder groups.

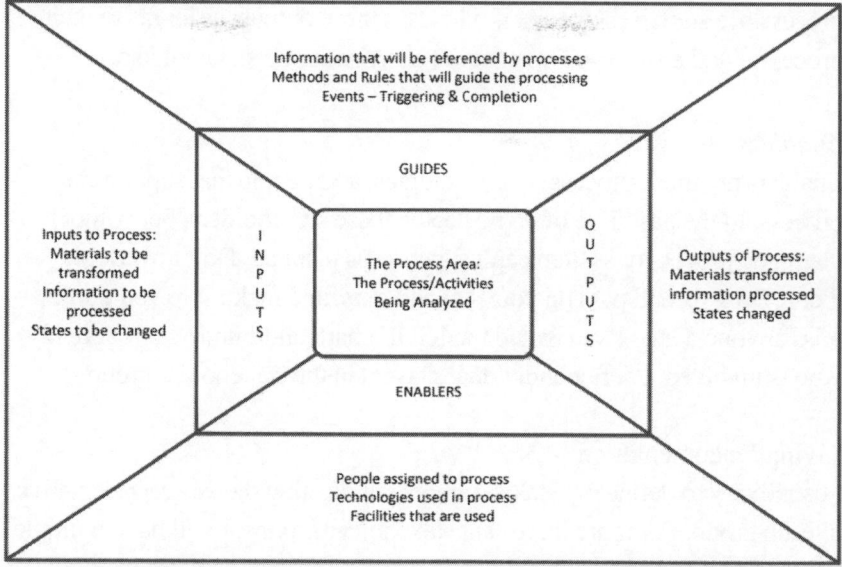

FIGURE 7. IGOE — Link to Decision Criteria (Long, 2012)

Inputs

Which processes and people provide inputs to the problem we're trying to address? In this section, I look to discover the triggers, people, and processes that kick off things in our system. The people who provide these inputs are important stakeholders and this tool allows me to better understand them.

Guidelines

These come from information and rules which govern the processes, including any business rules that govern the situation and anything that could trigger the process from starting or stopping, including regulatory bodies and laws. I need to understand their needs when I elicit requirements. They definitely need to be represented in my stakeholder analysis.

Outputs

All processes involve transforming some data, whether informational or material, whereby we take in raw data (inputs) and transform it into something else (outputs). Determining who is influenced by the output of the transformation helps define the stakeholders downstream from the process. Be sure to ask yourself who uses these outputs as inputs to their processes and ensure you've covered all your output stakeholders.

Enablers

Enablers are those processes, technologies, and people that support the process. In the past, I've often neglected these stakeholders, but without them, the process or system can't function as planned. Don't overlook them! Do a second pass on your stakeholders, and make sure you don't miss anyone. Once I've created the IGOE chart, and I understand roughly who is involved, I define individual players in the stakeholder group.

Living Documentation

I usually try to define my stakeholders by indicating the key representative in each group. For more important stakeholder groups, I will have multiple people listed, because even though they represent the same group, they might have differing attitudes and perspectives on the project.

Warning: The stakeholder analysis document is not to be shared with anyone. You will use this control document to ensure everyone is covered. Much of this information is sensitive, such as the attitudes of the stakeholders towards your project. You still need to manage those stakeholders without jeopardizing yourself. It could be dangerous to your career if anyone were to read that you believe the VP is a hostile stakeholder; even if it might be true, it doesn't help anyone or the project for your views to become public knowledge.

Group	Key Representative	Stakeholder Characteristics							
		Complexity	Attitude	Influence	Authority	Direct/Indirect Involvement	Relationship with / Interest in project	Goals / Success Criteria	Impact on Project	What does the project need from this group?

FIGURE 1: My Stakeholder Analysis Excel File

Group

There are many ways you can use this field, but I typically use organizational functions. I've learned that these groups are already well defined in the organization, and they've worked well for me in the past.

Key Representative
In certain groups, you want more than one key representative. If I know that some stakeholders will provide additional challenges, I make sure to include them in the document.

Complexity
How complex is the stakeholder in this project? I typically rank them from low to high, which allows me to determine how involved I need to make this stakeholder group in eliciting and managing requirements. Groups and individuals with higher levels of complexity need more communication and more effort.

Attitude
This characteristic is important in that it defines how the stakeholder views the project and its importance. It also determines any political undercurrents that could potentially undermine or aid the initiative. Your job is to both mitigate negative attitudes and harness the energy of positive ones.

Influence
The level of influence of a stakeholder also affects how you deal with him or her. Those who control budgets have more influence than those who don't. Influence, however, is not just about who controls the financials; underpinning political waves must also be navigated. Some business users command a lot of respect because of their domain knowledge, and they can influence the viewpoints of those around them.

Authority
What is their level of authority in the project? Unlike influence, this tends to follow the money trail, either by financial budgeting or through organizational hierarchies.

Involvement

This section defines the perceived involvement in the project of the stakeholder group. Note that it is perceived, and it can change during the project. This is a high-level view, and it is only directionally accurate.

Interest

What is their interest in the project? What is in it for them? This question is incredibly important because, as a business analyst, you need to focus on delivering solutions that provide value to the organization. By determining each group's interest, you should have a clear picture of what needs to happen for project success.

Success Criteria

Define what project success looks like for each stakeholder group and representatives in those groups. You will observe that some stakeholders have diametrically opposed success criteria. Your mission is to get the stakeholders to agree to common success criteria. I like to leverage those with influence and authority to help reach that consensus.

Impact

What is the stakeholder's impact on the project? His or her role and contributions are important pieces of information from which you need to get the most out of in your elicitation sessions.

Project Need

What does the project need from this group? We were looking at what is in it for the stakeholders; now let's flip that around and determine what is in it for the project. What do we need from them to make the project a success?

Documenting the stakeholders' characteristics is just the beginning of the process. This living document needs constant updating as the project unfolds. If you consistently work with many of the same stakeholders on projects, you will build a good understanding of their goals and objectives.

Requirements Work Plan

Now that we understand the players from whom we need to elicit
requirements, we can focus on defining how to proceed. In the
Requirements Work Plan, I determine how and when I will elicit
requirements from my stakeholders and the details required to make it
happen.

Schedule

Our first effort should be to determine the schedule for our sessions.
How many sessions will we need, and whom do we invite to each
session? This depends on how comfortable your stakeholders are with
you and with one another. Do they need to be segregated? Are there
clear delineations among stakeholder groups that allow you to break
them apart to make elicitation easier? There isn't a hard and fast rule on
this, unfortunately; it just depends.

I always try to minimize the disruption of my stakeholders; I try
very hard not to waste their time. The sessions need to be manageable,
and they need to impose as little as possible on the stakeholders' time.
Experience will help you determine what is best.

Format

It's time to plan your sessions. Where are they being held? What do
you wish to accomplish in each session, and who is invited to each?
Not all stakeholders are alike. I schedule interviews with the executive
stakeholders to get their viewpoints and give them more personal
attention to ensure their perspectives aren't overlooked.

I then document how the elicitation will unfold by answering the
six questions: who, what, when, where, why, and how. Event details
include booking the rooms, determining catering or props, booking
stakeholders' schedules, and creating and managing your agenda.

I like to understand the different components and features that might go into the new project so I can ask better and more informed questions. I define how the session will unfold so I can lead the stakeholders down the path to success. This doesn't always work the way I envisioned, but I'm well prepared to adapt to any necessary changes.

If you're not well prepared for an elicitation session, you will find they can be disastrous. Your sessions will quickly go sideways, and at the end of the session, you might find yourself asking what happened. Don't fall into that trap. Prepare for the sessions, and stay on target!

Clarification and Elaboration

I usually add a few more sessions as placeholders after the initial sessions for clarification and elaboration of the details. I use this time to clean up any issues that might have been parked during the initial sessions. I allocate extra time to achieve sign-off. As for the time I allocate for this ... well, that depends. Experience will be your guide, and I like to use the stakeholder analysis guide to help me define how long this needs to be. As more and more stakeholders move in the same direction and want the project to succeed, the less time you will need to allocate.

I always give myself extra contingency time. The length of the contingency is proportional to the risk involved in the requirements effort. Will the stakeholders be available when you need them? Are they taking holidays, or are they involved in other projects that might distract them from yours? The more likely this is, the more contingency I allow. When the plan is compiled and documented, I clean it up and present it to the project team. I proactively prepare the requirements plan, and then I do my utmost to stick to it.

I remember the first project for which I had my requirements work plan completed before the project manager asked for it. Rather than dictate when my requirements needed to be complete, we worked together to integrate my work plan into the overall project plan. The project ended up running very smoothly, and it's one of my most successful projects.

Learnings

A good friend of mine who was in the military often says that a plan is only good until first contact with the enemy. Your plan isn't a static document; it will change over your efforts. Adjust the schedule and the timelines as necessary, and be sure to communicate changes to your project team.

Learn from your plans. Through experience, you'll get to know how many sessions and how long each session needs to be. Do a mini look-back on your efforts and incorporate your learnings into your next plan. Through constant effort, you'll find that you will get better and better at planning.

Plan to Succeed!

The key to business analysis planning is to make sure that it is completed to the detail required, but do not go too deep. Don't overanalyze your plan, and understand that your plan needs to be flexible, and it will change. Adjust your plan as necessary, and focus on achieving value for your stakeholders.

A plan does not guarantee success, but the chance of success for those projects planned is exponentially higher than for those unplanned. Give yourself every chance to succeed.

Jared Gorai
M 403-612-4200
Twitter: @thepassionateba

Jared is a passionate business analyst currently contracting in Calgary, Alberta. He has been a business analyst in title for more than 10 years, although he's performed the role for much longer. He holds a Bachelor of Arts degree from the University of Calgary and the Certified Business Analysis Professional™ (CBAP®) designation. He is a past president of the Calgary IIBA® Chapter, and he loves to evangelize the role of the profession whenever possible.

References
Long, Kathy A. "IGOE — Link to Decision Criteria." *Business Rules Journal* 13, no. 5 (May 2012).
http://www.BRCommunity.com/a2012/b653.html

16

BA 3.0:
Thriving in the
Marketplace

Sohail Thaker

What does it take for a business analyst (BA) to do more than survive in the marketplace? What does it take for you to thrive?

From my experience, I have learned that being an "order taker" does not work. I remember a project for which I was hired to put in a new accounting system, and instead, I recommended changes to business processes and personnel that resulted in significant reductions in process time without any system changes. I was willing to take a risk and recommend what I thought would solve the problem, rather than "taking an order."

In my role as a partner at a consulting firm, I recognize that the best BAs make themselves indispensable, and are courageous problem solvers willing to challenge the status quo. To thrive, we can no longer be content with being average, delivering average solutions. To thrive, we must embrace our passion and creativity and challenge ourselves and our clients to develop unique solutions that help create a competitive advantage.

The Evolution of BAs

I have a background in software development, so when thinking of how to describe the evolution of BAs, I thought of the concept of version numbers. So, let's talk about the evolution of BAs as BA 1.0, BA 2.0, and BA 3.0.

BA 1.0—Travelling Without a Map

When I started my career more than 20 years ago as a BA, I worked for a software development firm in the UK that developed software for the healthcare market. This was an interesting time in a very young IT industry. The role of BA was not well defined. My role was to act as a liaison between the clients and the developers, documenting requirements and developing functional specifications.

My boss could not give me much direction, and instead asked me to "figure it out" and treated business analysis as a "black art." I had no access to the Internet (this was a long time ago…), and easy access to tools, guidelines, and templates was nonexistent. Without much guidance, I learned *on the fly*, making mistakes while learning how to capture requirements and communicate with both clients and developers. It was like traveling without a map. I would think on my feet, take risks, make decisions, and develop tools and approaches on my own, learning what worked and what didn't.

BA 2.0—Focus on Consistency

Fast forward 20 years, and we are in a very different world for BAs. The IIBA is now well established, and an extensive *BABOK* is available. The Internet is an easy source of tools, templates, and approaches that have proved successful. Companies have embraced project management and business analysis, and developed methodologies and structured processes BAs are expected to follow. The role of BA is more recognized, and business better understands the capabilities and value of BAs.

With this new (BA 2.0) environment, we can expect BAs to focus on being more consistent in their approach and deliverables, given they have access to the same tools, training and methodologies. BAs now follow the corporate checklists that define their expected deliverables.

What the Market Wants

In my role as partner at a business and information technology consulting firm in Calgary, I am fortunate to have access to executives responsible for business analysis at their organizations. I interviewed them to determine what they thought their BAs were failing to do. Here is a list of their complaints:

- Our BAs tend to focus on the detail too much and like being "stuck in the weeds."
- We want our BAs to be more top-down in their thinking, understanding the big picture first before dropping into the details.
- BAs are forgetting to think on their feet. The job is not simply about completing templates and documents. The tools are there to help you focus your thoughts.
- BAs should be more focused on delivering what is "good enough" than creating perfect documents.

- BAs can be "order takers," literally delivering what their clients ask for instead of challenging their clients to determine what problem needs to be solved.
- BAs are becoming rule followers, and they are not showing the leadership and courage their role requires.

Clearly, even with our evolution from BA 1.0 to BA 2.0, we are still missing what the market wants.

BA 3.0—Thriving

When we look at the evolution from BA 1.0 to BA 2.0, we can easily see what we gained. We established better standards, recognition for BAs, tools and templates, and the definition of techniques to ensure better BA consistency. But what did we lose in this evolution?

We lost some of the *art* of being a BA—the ability to think on our feet, adapt to new situations, and be creative. Consistency can be a good and a bad thing; BA 2.0 helped improve the baseline capability of all BAs, but it also made us a little lazy, turning many BAs into *rule followers* who met the expected criteria and deliverables but failed to introduce some creativity or challenge the expected process. Consistency raised the average capability of all BAs, but it did not encourage individuality and uniqueness, characteristics needed to develop unique, market leading solutions.

BA 3.0 is simply BA 2.0 plus some exceptional personal traits and skills. BA 3.0 assumes that you have mastered the tools available (BA 2.0) without losing some of the art of being a BA (BA 1.0). A BA 3.0 does not accept being average; he strives to be exceptional, unique, and indispensable. BAs who embrace BA 3.0 are leaders who are courageous and willing to be artists again. They are willing to travel without a map, while using all the techniques they have mastered. They look to do more than survive. They want to thrive, to be more than average, and help their clients do the same.

Be a Chef, Not a Cook

In my definition, cooks can prepare meals by following a recipe. Over time, they get better and better at following the recipe and strive to deliver consistent taste and appearance. Chefs do much more than this. Chefs have mastered the principles, techniques, and methodologies of cooking. They have gone to culinary school and put in their time in many kitchens, practicing their techniques so they, too, can deliver meals with consistent taste and appearance. Chefs then do something cooks do not; they apply their passion and creativity and start to use their mastery of the tools and techniques to create something unique and wonderful. Their aim is no longer consistency or following recipes; they aim for greatness, an experience their client will not forget. They aim to produce a work of art.

Many years ago, a client hired me to implement a database application to manage its drawing approval process. My first step was to analyze their existing process to understand where bottlenecks existed. In this analysis, I realized that putting in a database was not the answer; the client was trying to implement the wrong solution. Their processes had evolved as they grew from a small team that checked one another's work to a large organization with several departments checking the work. What had worked well in the small team no longer made sense in the larger organization.

I designed a new business process that maintained quality while removing many unnecessary and inefficient steps. I presented my approach to the CEO with my recommendation to discard the database implementation. He was shocked, and he quickly realized that my suggestions made sense. Instead of being a *cook* and simply doing what the client requested, I challenged the client's assumption of wanting a new information system and identified their issue as being about saving time.

My job as a BA, as in my example of being a chef, was to use my skills creatively and courageously to find the most efficient way to save time, regardless of what the client thought the solution should be. This resulted in the client successfully implementing the changes and achieving significant time savings.

BAs (BA 2.0) who think like cooks follow the *recipes* in the *BABOK* to deliver consistent work—but there is little unique about the solutions they develop. BAs (BA 3.0) who think like chefs see recipes as a starting point, but they are also willing to put something of themselves into their work, expressing their passion, creativity, and art. This approach is not without risk, and in some cases, chefs fail. However, without the courage to risk and willingness to fail and learn, we are unlikely to create something unique that delivers a competitive advantage for the client.

We Don't Need Faster Horses

BAs who embrace BA 3.0 should constantly ask themselves, "How am I adding value?" As BAs, we should constantly evaluate how we can help move a project along. We should check to see whether we are following the process too closely. Are we challenging the value of the (expected) steps we are prescribed to take? Sometimes, following the process/methodology does not make sense. We should look for opportunities to drop low-value work so we can focus on high-value activities.

If no one on your team is waiting anxiously for your deliverable, you should wonder why you are working on it. I can think of many projects in which I would question the need to create a specific document if I knew that no team member needed the document, even when the "official processes" defined it was "needed."

I know that, sometimes, we need to create documents for compliance purposes, but in these cases, I would do the bare minimum rather than spend my energy creating a *work of art*. My focus was to put my energy on documents and deliverables that helped the team and the project move forward, to keep my focus on delivery as opposed to meeting the checklist of defined documents.

When we interact with our clients, we need to be willing to challenge them rather than be an order taker. Henry Ford is credited with saying, "If I'd asked people what they wanted, they would have asked for faster horses." The job of the BA is to challenge the client, to get to the root of their needs, rather than simply transcribing their stated requirements. We should be prepared to ask questions, to promote different approaches, and to be an artist in how we develop a solution. We are not here to create a specification for "faster horses," we are here to deliver a unique solution to move from point A to point B faster. BAs who take this approach add value and make themselves indispensable to their organizations.

Conclusion

With the advent of BA 2.0, we introduced consistency, standards, and techniques that raised the bar for all BAs, but we created a new average. We lost some creativity and risk taking, and the ability to work without the map we had in BA 1.0. To thrive, we can no longer be content with being average, delivering average solutions.

BA 3.0 aims to address the complaints about BAs becoming order takers. I encourage you to become an artist again, to be a chef, to risk failure, and to create great works of art, instead of faster horses. Most BAs are natural problem solvers with a talent for coming up with creative solutions, whether at work or in your personal life. BA 3.0 aims to rekindle that passion and allow you to express it again through your work. By doing so, you will find more energy and creativity in your work. You will thrive and become an indispensable asset to your organization. I challenge you to embrace BA 3.0 and be the BA you always knew you could be.

Sohail Thaker
Ethier
E-mail: sthaker@ethier.ca
Website: www.ethier.ca
LinkedIn: Sohail Thaker

Sohail is a partner at Ethier, a Calgary-based consulting firm. In a career spanning almost three decades, Sohail has worked in Africa, India, and Europe. Before joining the Ethier Partnership, he was a consultant with Ethier for 12 years. Sohail's résumé includes project management (traditional, Agile, and Scrum), business analysis, business process innovation, organizational change management, and facilitation.

Ethier is a premier consulting firm that drives business excellence. For over 30 years, they have helped their clients realize their strategic goals with a focus on managing change, improving portfolios, facilitating program and project delivery, and achieving operational excellence. Their senior consultants bring a blend of experience, business acumen, and domain expertise to deliver business initiatives that consistently meet or exceed clients' expectations. Ethier works in collaboration with clients to adapt and prioritize efforts to meet business and project-specific needs and ensure a *fit-for-purpose* approach that delivers the desired benefits.

Ethier was recognized as one of "Canada's Best Managed Companies" in 2012, and re-qualified in 2013.
Sohail's accomplishments:

- MBA in International Business
- Certified Project Management Professional (PMP) with the Project Management Institute
- Prosci ADKAR certified
- Sohail in real life:

- Star Trek geek, Star Wars nerd, and zombie aficionado, with a dog named Wookiee
- Practices Iaido, the Japanese martial art of drawing the sword
- A born-again runner who has moved from 10K distances to half-marathons and ran his first marathon in June 2014.
- Involved in personal development workshops and facilitates and provides counseling

17

A Business Analyst Is a Key Agent of Innovation

Paskwa Mutunga

One of the greatest lessons I've learned is that a business analyst's role goes beyond *gathering and documenting functional and nonfunctional requirements.* A business analyst is a key agent of innovation.

I love to watch the TV show *One House, Two Looks*, hosted by Jane Lockhart and Jason Cass. I find it fascinating that Jane and Jason can create two different great looks for identical houses. Several years ago, I had an experience with two projects that felt a bit like *One House Two Looks*. The only difference was that instead of getting two great looks, one was great, whereas the other was—well—not so good. I have since code-named these projects—Project Strawberry and

Project Lemon.

Lemon and Strawberry were similar in many ways—both were innovation projects, both used an ad-hoc Agile approach, and both required the team to engage with the same offshore vendor. But Project Lemon was stressful, confusing, exhausting and laden with conflict and blame games, while Project Strawberry was relaxed, refreshing, and fun.

What caused the difference? The biggest difference was that Project Strawberry involved developing a new technology tool for an established product offering, whereas Project Lemon involved creating a new product offering as well as the technology platform for it. Project Lemon required a different set of business analysis skills—the ability to help the client crystallize an innovative concept and evolve it into a revenue-generating product, which helped me learn that a business analyst is a key agent of innovation.

Traditional vs. Ad Hoc Agile Project Approach

Our organization had recently adopted innovation as a major strategic focus. As a result, our team was encouraged to shift from the traditional project approach to Agile. In the traditional project approach, project phases were well defined and carried out sequentially starting with initiation, requirements, design construction, testing, and production rollout. Each phase had a well-defined set of deliverables used as input in the next phase (See Figure 9).

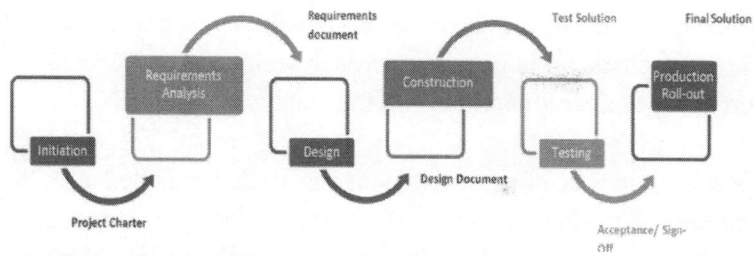

FIGURE. 9. Traditional Project Approach

In the ad-hoc agile approach we adopted, the project phases were not managed sequentially. Our stakeholders expected us to define high-level requirements, prioritize them, allocate them to releases, and start development in short time intervals called "sprints." Figure 10 illustrates our ad-hoc Agile approach.

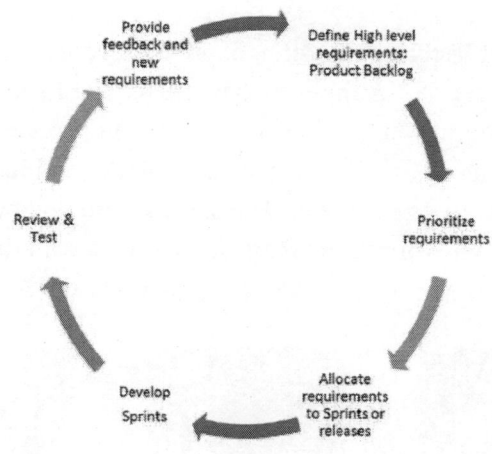

FIGURE 10. Our Ad-hoc Agile Approach

Project Strawberry was a small project with a team of five that included a product owner, project manager, business analyst, developer, and tester. The scope of the project was to develop an innovative mobile application for an existing business product offering. The requirements were simple—a list of cool features and a user interface for the application. The product backlog was well defined, features were prioritized, and development started. Sprints were brief with a release of the mobile application every two weeks. The application was tested, and we incorporated feedback into the next sprint. This simplistic ad-hoc Agile approach seemed to work for Strawberry. We delivered on time, and the team was happy.

Project Lemon was a big project with a team that included a project sponsor, a business owner, a solution architect, a creative team, five developers, three testers, a project manager, a business analyst, a designer, and the marketing team. The scope of the project was to create a new product offering and build a technology platform that integrated with several existing systems. The business analyst's key role was to define functional and nonfunctional requirements for the technical solution. The business owner and the marketing team were assigned the task of developing the new product offering.

The product backlog was defined, prioritized, and allocated to sprints for the user facing applications. The requirements for the technology platform were defined for seven major solution components, each on a different system illustrated in Figure 11. Sprints were released every three weeks. The sprints were reviewed in the development environment, and they did not include all the integration pieces.

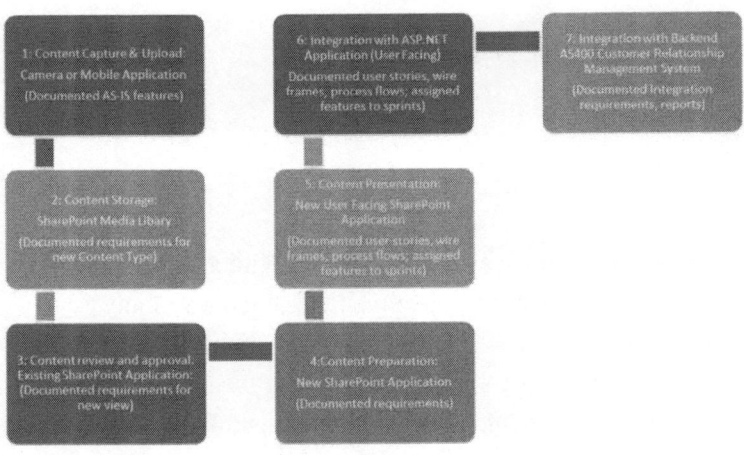

FIGURE 11. Project Lemon Integration

We had three application environments: development, staging, and production. Developers did initial development and debugging in development. We then promoted the application to staging for quality assurance and user acceptance testing. When testing was completed, we promoted the application to production. Ideally, each environment should have been identical, or at least, the staging environment should have been identical to the production environment. Unfortunately, each environment was different.

When we promoted the technical solution for Project Lemon to staging for user acceptance testing, the integration did not work as expected. It took one month to get all the systems communicating as expected. When we promoted the solution to production, we encountered new issues we could not reproduce in any other environment. Resolving the issues was compounded by the time difference among the developers in Asia, the developers in Canada, and the operation support team in the United States. The team worked hard, and thanks to their determination and stubborn resilience, the solution finally worked as expected—two months later!

What Went Wrong? A Limited BA Role

The development of the new product offering was assigned to a business owner. Over the course of the project, several people were assigned the role of business owner. The new product concept was appealing; however, it was not clearly defined. Every business owner understood the concept differently, which led to several major changes.

When Project Lemon's technical solution was finally up and running, a new business owner was assigned. The new business owner decided to target a different customer segment and change the key messaging and value proposition. These business strategy changes resulted in additional changes; we received a new request to change the product name, key features, and the entire user experience. At this point, the fights and blame games began. The team's stress levels were high, and some team members stopped showing up to status meetings. This lemon was getting bitter!

The biggest lesson I learned from Project Lemon and Project Strawberry is that for any project, the business analyst's role is not limited to requirements gathering for functional and nonfunctional requirements. A business analyst can go beyond these roles and help the business develop an innovation strategy for a new product, clarify business goals, and develop a business model, which is what made Project Strawberry and Lemon so radically different. Project Strawberry's business needs, scope, and requirements were well defined because the product offering already existed; Project Lemon? Quite the opposite.

The greatest challenge of Project Lemon was that the business need was not well defined. The new product was defined conceptually. However, the value proposition, customer segments, key activities, long-term and short-term strategy, and general messaging for the new product were not defined. Throughout the project, I recognized the gaps. I launched company-wide training on enterprise analysis. I intended to give others the knowledge so they could create better business cases. It hadn't crossed my mind that it would have been OK for me to go beyond the role of "gathering and documenting functional and nonfunctional requirements" to being an agent of innovation for Project Lemon.

The BA as Key Innovation Agent

When I look back, it would have made a big difference if I had stepped up and played the role of key innovation agent. I could have done this three ways. First, I would have helped clarify the business need, desired outcome, and SMART goals for the new product offering. Second, I would have helped the business crystallize the new product concept into a tangible business model. Third, I would have asked questions to clarify and challenge assumptions about the integration requirements for the technical solution.

Clarify the Business Need

Let's look at the first point—help clarify the business need, desired outcome, and SMART goals for the project. The business problem or opportunity Project Lemon dealt with was not clear to all stakeholders. As a business analyst, I could have facilitated communication to ensure common understanding of the business need, solution approach, and scope.

To clarify the business need, I could have asked these simple questions:

- What needs to be done? What business need or opportunity does this project address? What's the desired outcome? What strategy and SMART goal will the business adopt to get to the desired outcome? The responses to these questions form the business need.

- Who will do it? This leads me to the stakeholders—the people involved in executing the project or those affected by it. Ideally, each SMART goal needs to be assigned to at least one person.

- How will it be done? This helps me identify processes that will change, or new processes that will be required. The platform could include technology or any other tools that will be used to meet the business goal.

FIGURE 12. Clarify the Business Need

Crystallize the Product Concept

The second approach would have been to help the business crystallize the new product concept into a viable business model. When I conducted the enterprise analysis training, one participant introduced me to an amazing business-modeling tool, the Business Model Canvas by Alexander Osterwalder. The Business Model Canvas is holistic, and it helps map a business model for an innovative idea. It has nine building blocks summarized in the diagram below.

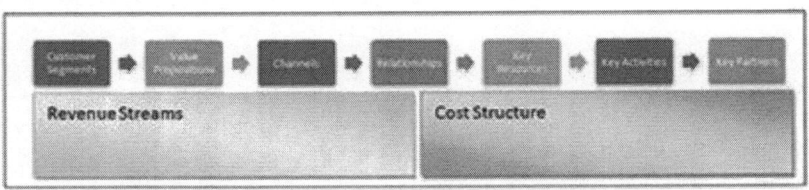

FIGURE 13. Business Model Canvas Building Blocks

A business analyst can start by helping the business identify the customer segment they target. You can then walk the business through figuring out what value proposition they will create for that customer segment, the channels they will use to get the value proposition to the customer, and the relationships they will form. Once completed, the tool gives an idea of the revenue the business can expect to raise and the costs associated with creating the value proposition for that customer segment.

This tool's beauty is that in a very short time, a business analyst can facilitate a session in which the stakeholders can map their complete business model in a visual and interactive way. This is a must-have tool for any business analyst who wants to go beyond gathering and documenting requirements to being a key agent of innovation. More information about the Business Model Canvas is available at http://www.businessmodelgeneration.com

Foster Creative Thinking

The third way a business analyst can play the role of innovation agent is by asking questions that encourage creative thinking by the team. When documenting a business process, ask why each step is required. Clarify and challenge assumptions. The biggest assumption we made in Project Lemon was that integration with all seven systems was required from the beginning. We later learned it would have been OK to integrate with one system and add the other interfaces progressively. If only we had asked more questions and clarified and challenged assumptions!

Though Project Lemon was not considered a success, I'm thankful for the lesson I learned—a business analyst is a key agent of innovation.

Paskwa Mutunga
E-mail: paskwa.mutunga@gmail.com
Twitter: @PaskwaMutunga

Paskwa Mutunga is passionate about equipping and empowering organizations to embrace change and implement creative, innovative technology strategies that propel and accelerate growth, save money, and increase productivity. Paskwa enjoys driving innovation using the Business Model Canvas and Lean Startup techniques.

She has over 20 years proven experience in leading diverse teams in the implementation of strategic technology solutions, distributed networks, and innovation frameworks; as well as managing the design, delivery, and refinement of training programs in Innovation, Business Analysis and Project Management.

Communication and Leadership

"Think like a wise man but communicate in the language of the people." - William Butler Yeats

"The best executive is the one who has sense enough to pick good men to do what he wants done, and self-restraint enough to keep from meddling with them while they do it." – Theodore Roosevelt

Will the Real Business Analysts (BAs) Please Stand Up—Building a Capable Business Analysis Team

Kathleen B. (Kitty) Hass

To say that a successful business analysis practice requires a team of capable, credible BAs is somewhat of an understatement. Being capable in business analysis practices is not enough in this complex, global world in which we now live. As the complexity of projects increases, BAs need to be accomplished, perhaps gifted, strategic thinkers and leaders of change the first step in determining the optimal make-up of your business analysis team is to determine the type and complexity of work they are and will be performing.

Step 1: Assess the Complexity of Project Assignments

Before you begin to build your business analysis team, assess the current project portfolio and backlog of potential projects for the next 12-to-18 months. The goal is to categorize projects according to their complexity. Let's get started! Using the Project Complexity Model 2.0 depicted below in Table 4, determine the profile of each project by selecting the cell that best describes the project for each complexity dimension, and then apply the formula following the model in Table 5.

Table 4. Project Complexity Model 2.0

Complexity Dimensions	Project Profile			
	Level 1: Low Complexity Project	Level 2: Moderately Complex Project	Level 3: Highly Complex Project	Level 4: Highly Complex Program "Megaproject"
1,Size/Time/Cost	Size: 3–4 team members Time: < 3 months Cost: < $250K	Size: 5–10 team members Time: 3–6 months Cost: $250–$1M	Size: > 10 team members Time: 6 – 12 months Cost: > $1M	Size: Multiple diverse teams Time: Multi-year Cost: Multiple Millions
2.Team Composition and Past Performance	• PM/BA: competent, experienced • Team: internal; worked together in past • Methodology: defined, proven	• PM/BA: competent, inexperienced • Team: internal and external, worked together in past • Methodology: defined, unproven • Contracts: straightforward • Contractor	• PM/BA: competent; poor/no experience with complex projects • Team: internal and external, have not worked together in past • Methodology: somewhat defined,	• PM/BA: competent, poor/no experience with megaprojects • Team: complex structure of varying competencies and performance records (e.g., contractor, virtual, culturally

Complexity Dimensions	Project Profile			
	Level 1: Low Complexity Project	Level 2: Moderately Complex Project	Level 3: Highly Complex Project	Level 4: Highly Complex Program "Megaproject"
		Past Performance: good	diverse • Contracts: complex • Contractor Past Performance: unknown	diverse, outsourced teams) • Methodology: undefined, diverse Contracts: highly complex • Contractor Past Performance: poor
3.Urgency and Flexibility of Cost, Time, and Scope	• Scope: minimized • Milestones: small • Schedule/Budget: flexible	• Scope: achievable • Milestones: achievable • Schedule/Budget: minor variations	• Scope: over-ambitious • Milestones: over-ambitious, firm • Schedule/Budget: inflexible	• Scope: aggressive • Milestones: aggressive, urgent • Schedule/Budget: aggressive
4.Clarity of Problem, Opportunity, Solution	• Objectives: defined and clear • Opportunity/Solution: easily understood	• Objectives: defined, unclear • Opportunity/Solution: partially understood	• Objectives: defined, ambiguous • Opportunity/Solution: ambiguous	• Objectives: undefined, uncertain • Opportunity/Solution: undefined, groundbreaking, unprecedented

Complexity Dimensions	Project Profile			
	Level 1: Low Complexity Project	Level 2: Moderately Complex Project	Level 3: Highly Complex Project	Level 4: Highly Complex Program "Megaproject"
5. Requirements Volatility and Risk	• Customer Support: strong • Requirements: understood, straightforward, stable • Functionality: straightforward	• Customer Support: adequate • Requirements: understood, unstable • Functionality: moderately complex	• Customer Support: unknown • Requirements: poorly understood, volatile • Functionality: highly complex	• Customer Support: inadequate • Requirements: uncertain, evolving • Functionality: many complex "functions of functions"
6. Strategic Importance, Political Implications, Stakeholders	• Executive Support: strong • Political Implications: none • Communications: straightforward • Stakeholder Management: straightforward	• Executive Support: adequate • Political Implications: minor • Communications: challenging • Stakeholder Management: 2–3 stakeholder groups	• Executive Support: inadequate • Political Implications: major, impacts core mission • Communications: complex • Stakeholder Management: multiple stakeholder groups with conflicting expectations; visible at high levels of the	• Executive Support: unknown • Political Implications: impacts core mission of multiple programs, organizations, states, countries; success critical for competitive or physical survival • Communications: arduous • Stakeholder Management:

Complexity Dimensions	Project Profile			
	Level 1: Low Complexity Project	Level 2: Moderately Complex Project	Level 3: Highly Complex Project	Level 4: Highly Complex Program "Megaproject"
			organization	multiple organizations, states, countries, regulatory groups; visible at high internal and external levels
7. Level of Change	Organizational Change: impacts a single business unit, one familiar business process, and one IT system Commercial Change: no changes to existing commercial practices	Organizational Change: impacts 2–3 familiar business units, processes, and IT systems Commercial Change: enhancements to existing commercial practices	Organizational Change: impacts the enterprise, spans functional groups or agencies; shifts or transforms many business processes and IT systems Commercial Change: new commercial and cultural practices	Organizational Change: impacts multiple organizations, states, countries; transformative new venture Commercial Change: ground-breaking commercial and cultural practices
8. Risks, Dependencies, and External Constraints	Risk Level: low External Constraints: no external influences	Risk Level: moderate External Constraints: some external factors	Risk Level: high External Constraints: key objectives depend on	Risk Level: very high External Constraints: project success depends largely

Complexity Dimensions	Project Profile			
	Level 1: Low Complexity Project	Level 2: Moderately Complex Project	Level 3: Highly Complex Project	Level 4: Highly Complex Program "Megaproject"
	Integration: no integration issues Potential Damages: no punitive exposure	Integration: challenging integration effort Potential Damages: acceptable exposure	external factors Integration: significant integration required Potential Damages: significant exposure	on multiple external organizations, states, countries, regulators Integration: unprecedented integration effort Potential Damages: unacceptable exposure
9. Level of IT Complexity	• Technology: technology is proven and well-understood • IT Complexity: application development and legacy integration easily understood	• Technology: technology is proven but new to the organization • IT Complexity: application development and legacy integration largely understood	• Technology: technology is likely to be immature, unproven, complex, and provided by outside vendors • IT Complexity: application development and legacy integration poorly understood	• Technology: technology requires groundbreaking innovation and unprecedented engineering accomplishments • IT Complexity: multiple "systems of systems" to be developed and integrated

Source: Project Complexity Model 2.0. ©2009 by Kathleen Hass and Associates, Inc. (Hass, 2009)

Table 5. Project Complexity Formula

Highly Complex Program "Megaproject"	Highly Complex Project	Moderately Complex	Independent
Size: Multiple diverse teams Time: Multi-year Cost: Multiple Millions Or 2 or more in the Highly Complex Program/Megaproject column	Organizational Change: impacts the enterprise, spans functional groups or agencies, shifts or transforms many business processes and IT systems Or 3 or more categories in the Highly Complex Project column And No more than 1 category in the Highly Complex Program/Megaproject column	3 or more categories in the Moderately Complex Project column Or No more than 2 categories in the Highly Complex Project column and	No more than 2 categories in the Moderately Complex Project column And No categories in the Highly Complex Project or the Highly Complex Program/Megaproject column

Project Complexity Model 2.0. ©2009 by Kathleen Hass and Associates, Inc. adapted from *Managing Complex Projects: A New Model* by Kathleen B. Hass (Vienna VA, Management Concepts, Inc.). All rights reserved. www.managementconcepts.com/pubs

Business Analysis Book of Mentors

Step 2: Determine the mix of BAs needed to build your Capable BA Workforce

Obviously, the skills required by both PMs and BAs differ widely depending on the complexity profile of their project assignments. Referring to the BA Individual/Workforce Capability Model below, determine the number of BAs needed at each level of complexity to successfully execute current and anticipated projects at each level of the model. From this information, you are ready to begin to build your BA team. The model is four-tiered for both project managers and business analysts as described below. The levels of the model are based on the escalating complexity of typical project assignments, as follows:

TABLE 6: Areas of Focus

Level	Area of Focus	Complexity Profile	Business Outcomes
1.	Operations and Support Projects	Low Complexity	Business operations are maintained and enhanced
2.	Project Focused Projects	Moderately Complex	Business objectives are met through projects
3.	Enterprise Projects	Highly Complex Projects	Business strategy is executive through projects, programs and portfolios
4.	Competitive Projects	Highly Complex Programs	New business strategy is forged and competitive advantage is improved through innovation and business/technology optimization

Level 1: Operations and Support Focus

To maintain and enhance business operations, both generalists and system specialists are needed. These BAs typically spend about 30% of their time doing business analysis activities for low complexity projects designed to maintain and continually improve business processes and technology. The remaining time they are often fulfilling multiple roles including developer, engineer, SME, domain expert, and tester. As legacy processes and systems age, these BAs are becoming more valuable since they are likely the best (and often the *only*) SMEs who understand the current business processes and supporting technology. Many organizations are creating separate groups of PMs, BAs and developers to manage maintenance of current business processes, the legacy systems that support them, and the vendors who are engaged to help support the legacy IT operations.

Level 2: Project Focus
To ensure business objectives are met through projects, both IT- and Business-Oriented BAs are needed. These BAs work on moderately complex projects designed to develop new/improved business processes and IT systems.

- IT-Oriented BAs improve operations through changes to technology. The BAs are mostly generalists, with specialists that include Experience Analysts, Business Rules Analysts, Business Process Analysts, Data Analysts, etc.

- Business-Oriented BAs improve operations through changes to policy and procedures. Business-oriented BAs are mostly specialized, focused on Finance, Human Resources, Marketing, Manufacturing, etc. In decentralized organizations, these BAs are dedicated to a major business area, improving the processes and the corresponding technologies that are used to run the operations. In other more centralized organizations, these BAs are organized as a pool of talent whose efforts can be transferred seamlessly to the areas of the enterprise that are in most need of project suppor

Business Analyst (BA) Workforce Capability Model

1. Operations / Support Focus	2. Project Focus	3. Enterprise Focus	4. Competitive Focus
PROJECTS	**PROJECTS**	**PROJECTS**	**PROJECTS**
Low complexity projects that continually enhance business processes, products, or technologies	Moderately complex new development projects that improve business processes, products, or technologies	Highly complex projects that improve several business processes, products, or technologies	Highly complex innovation programs that improve competitive advantage and translate strategy into breakthrough processes and technologies
OUTCOMES	**OUTCOMES**		**OUTCOMES**
Value of operational business process and systems is continually enhanced	Business requirements and project scope are managed to ensure new solutions meet business objectives	**OUTCOMES** The enterprise is investing in the most valuable initiatives and is realizing the business benefits forecast in the business case	New strategy formulated. Business/techn ology optimized. Improved competitive position.
TYPE OF LEADER Generalists, business/syste m specialists, product managers	**TYPE OF LEADER** Business domain experts, IT system experts	**TYPE OF LEADER** Enterprise change experts, business architects	**TYPE OF LEADER** Strategists, business/techn ology optimization experts, innovation & cultural change experts, R&D Consultants, enterprise and business/ technology optimization BAs
Entry-level and senior BAs	Entry-level and senior BAs	Senior and enterprise BAs	

Continuous Advancement of Competence, Credibility, Creativity, and Influence

FIGURE 14. Business Analyst (BA) Workforce Capability Model

Level 3: Enterprise Focus

This group includes very seasoned PMs and BAs. PMs are trained and experienced in managing highly complex projects, programs and portfolios. The BAs often specialize into two groups: Enterprise Analysts and Business Architects, who are operating at the strategic level of the organization ensuring that the business analysis activities are dedicated to the most valuable initiatives, and the business analysis assets (deliverables/artifacts e.g., models, diagrams) are considered corporate assets and are therefore reusable. Enterprise PMs and BAs focus on the analysis needed to prepare a solid business case to propose new initiatives and work on highly-complex enterprise-wide projects; while Business Architects make the enterprise visible and keep the business and IT architectures in synch.

Level 4: Competitive Focus

Business/Technology Optimization BAs are business and technology visionaries who serve as Innovation Experts, Organizational Change Specialists, and Cross Domain Experts. Business/Technology BAs focus outside of the enterprise on what the industry is doing and design innovative new approaches to doing business to ensure the enterprise remains competitive, or even leaps ahead of the competition. Business/Technology BAs forge new strategies, translate strategy into breakthrough process and technology, and convert business opportunities to innovative business solutions.

The capabilities that are needed at each level of the model differ significantly. BA technical capabilities are needed at every level; leadership and soft skill competencies and techniques are needed to succeed on higher-level, more complex projects. See below for a listing of capabilities and techniques needed to perform successfully at each level of the model.

Table 6. Business Analyst (BA) Technical Capabilities

BA Technical Capabilities
See BABOK® Guide for detailed descriptions of the tasks, activities, and techniques used for each capability

Project Focused

1. Business Analysis Planning and Monitoring
2. Elicitation
3. Requirements Management and Communication
4. Requirements Analysis

Enterprise Focused

5. Enterprise Analysis
6. Solution Assessment and Validation

Table 7. Business Analyst (BA) Competencies and Techniques

BA COMPETENCIES AND TECHNIQUES USED TO PERFORM THE WORK	
Operations/Support-Focused Business Analyst	
1. Acceptance and Evaluation Criteria Definition	12. Observation
2. Brainstorming	13. Problem Tracking
3. Checklists	14. Re-planning
4. Continuous Process Improvement	15. Requirements Change Management
5. Defect and Issue Reporting	16. Requirements Documentation
6. Document Analysis	17. Requirements Prioritization
7. Estimation	18. Sequence Diagramming
8. Functional Decomposition	19. Stakeholder Analysis/Mapping
9. Interface Analysis	20. Time Boxing / Budgeting
10. Interviews	21. Voting
11. Non-Functional Requirements Analysis	
Project-Focused Business Analyst	
1. Baselining	22. Requirements Briefings and Presentations
2. Business Case Validation	23. Requirements for Vendor Selection
3. Business Process Analysis and Management	24. Requirements Traceability/Coverage Matrix
4. Business Rules Analysis and Management	25. Requirements Decomposition
5. Change Management	26. Requirements Workshops
6. Conflict and Issue Management	27. Requirements Review, Validation and Signoff
7. Consensus Mapping	28. Responsibility Matrix (RACI)
8. Communications Requirements Analysis	29. Reverse Engineering
9. Business Process Design	30. RFI, RFQ, RFP
10. Data Dictionary and Glossary	31. Risk Analysis
11. Data Flow Diagrams	32. Scenarios and Use Cases
12. Data Modeling	33. Scope Modeling
13. Decision Analysis	
14. Delphi	

15. Expert Judgment
16. Focus Groups
17. Force Field Analysis
18. MoSCoW Analysis
19. Process Modeling
20. Prototyping
21. Requirements Attribute Assignment

34. Solution Modeling
35. State Diagrams
36. Structured Walkthroughs
37. Survey/Questionnaire
38. User Acceptance Testing
39. User Stories and Storyboards
40. Value Analysis
41. Variance Analysis
42. Vendor Assessment

Enterprise-Focused Business Analyst

1. Balanced Scorecard
2. Benchmarking
3. Business Architecture
4. Business Case Development and Validation
5. Business Opportunity Analysis
6. Business Problem Analysis
7. Business Process Reengineering
8. Competitive Analysis
9. Cost/Benefit Analysis and Economic Modeling
10. Current State Analysis
11. Feasibility Analysis

12. Future State Analysis
13. Goal Decomposition
14. Gap Analysis
15. Last Responsible Moment Decision making
16. Lessons Learned Process
17. Metrics and Key Performance Indicators
18. Organizational Modeling
19. Organizational Change
20. Portfolio Analysis
21. Project and Program Prioritization
22. Root Cause Analysis (Fishbone Diagram)
23. SWOT Analysis

Business/Technology-Focused Business Analyst

1. Breakthrough Process Design
2. Cultural Change
3. Divergent thinking
4. Edge-of-Chaos Analysis
5. Emotional Intelligence
6. Experimentation
7. Idea Generation
8. Innovation and Creativity
9. Innovation Teams

10. Intuition
11. Investigation and Experimentation
12. Metaphors and Storytelling
13. Mind Mapping
14. Pattern Discovery
15. Research and Development
16. Strategic Planning
17. Systematic Inventive Thinking
18. Visualization

Building Your Capable Business Analyst (BA) Workforce for Levels 1 and 2: Low to Moderately Complex Projects

Take an inventory of the individuals currently serving in the BA role on your projects. Most will likely be operating at the first two levels of the model, focusing on requirements discovery and definition. This is the core business analysis function. Defining, analyzing, and documenting requirements is a highly creative and iterative process that is designed to show *what* the new/changed business system will do, and explore options for *how* it will be done. Therefore, the requirements in their textual and graphical form represent a depiction of the system, serving as an intermediate step between the business need and the solution design. The requirements development process is typically subdivided into *business need identification, scope definition, elicitation, analysis, specification, documentation, validation, management,* and *maintenance and enhancements.* These sub-disciplines encompass all the activities involved with gathering, evaluating, and documenting requirements (Young, 2001).

Don't fall into the trap of believing that expertise in the technical area of the project is the key requirement for the position of business analyst. In this case, business analysis is treated as a subset of the technical discipline. Time and again, projects encounter difficulties not from lack of technical expertise, but from an inability to gather, understand, analyze and manage business requirements, and convert them into useable system specifications. Projects are often initiated, and design and construction of the solution is underway, before IT team members have a clear understanding of the business need. Often, tolerance is low for technical failure and high for inadequate and ever-evolving requirements. All too often, projects suffer from requirements creep due to the "Let's start coding and see how it turns out" syndrome.

Look for candidates (both in the business areas and in IT) that understand that business requirements analysis differs from traditional information systems analysis because of its focus, which is exclusively on *adding value to the business*. In particular, build a BA team that focuses on providing more detailed project objectives; business needs analysis; clear, structured, useable requirements; trade-off analysis; solution feasibility and risk analysis; and cost-benefit analysis.

To build a team of capable BAs, technically adept engineers often are asked to make the professional transition to the disciplines of project management and business analysis. Often, these individuals assume a trio of leadership roles on projects: technical lead, project manager, and business analyst. Inevitably, after requirements are captured at a high level and the project plan is being executed, technical activities tend to elicit the majority of attention. When that happens, requirements and project management suffer, and the initiative is positioned to become a runaway project.

Research shows that there are still gaps in capabilities for BAs operating at levels 1 and 2. Assess the capabilities of the BAs you recruit, identify gaps, and create and execute a learning an development plan to close the gaps. To close gaps that exist on current projects, you may need to solicit experienced consultant BAs to ensure project success.

Build Your Strategic Business Analyst (BA) Workforce for Levels 3 and 4: Highly Complex Programs and Projects

It is increasingly clear that while technical BA knowledge areas are necessary, they are insufficient for successfully managing requirements on the large, enterprise-wide, complex, mission-critical projects that are the norm today. Just as a business leader must be multi-skilled and strategically focused, business analysts operating at the strategic level must possess an extensive array of leadership skills. As your BA Practice matures, recruit systems-thinking business analysts capable of assuming a leadership role on critical projects, and quickly elevate them to senior positions within the your BA team. As the IT contribution moves beyond efficiency to business success, the business analyst becomes the central figure on the project team who must be "bi-lingual" in speaking both business and technical languages. To perform in this pivotal role, the business analyst must possess a broad range of knowledge and skills. Browsing through the more than 5,000 job postings for business analysts on *Monster.com* turned up this job description:

> "The main purpose of the role will be to design and specify innovative solutions which meet the business requirements allowing the business benefit to be attained; and to facilitate divisional communication and awareness of the standards and quality expectations within the System Analyst teams."

Clearly, individuals performing business analysis activities at the strategic level do not always consider themselves part of the BA career family. But make no mistake; this is the path for the talented and ambitious business analyst. Look for individuals who have leadership qualities, are well respected, and carry influence within your organization to fill these most important BA roles.

Will the Real Business Analyst (BA) Please Stand Up

Many job titles exist for individuals performing BA activities, including business analyst, business systems analyst, business system planner, business architect, business rules analysts, and even principal solutions architect to name a few. Regardless of the job title, a strong, experienced business analyst is critical to complex project success. It has been said that if an organization only has resources and budget to put into a single life cycle area to improve project performance, that area should be business analysis. Depending on the level of responsibility and placement in the organization, business analyst duties at all levels include the following:

- Identify and understand the business problem and the impact of the proposed solution on the organization's operations
- Document the complex areas of project scope, objectives, added value or benefit expectations, using an integrated set of analysis and modeling techniques
- Translate business objectives into system requirements using powerful analysis and modeling tools
- Evaluate customer business needs, thus contributing to strategic planning of information systems and technology directions
- Assist in determining the strategic direction of the organization
- Liaise with major customers during preliminary installation and testing of new products and services
- Design and develop high quality business solutions

While the business analyst is fast becoming a relatively senior position in the business world, historically it has been considered a mid- to low-level role. A recent survey revealed an increasing demand for senior individuals who can perform the ever-widening range of business analysis functions. Since business analysts walk in both business and IT worlds, they will arrive to your team from various fields. Some come from the ranks of programmer/analyst positions, while others have conventional business expertise supplemented by some IT training. To successfully fill the business analyst role, one must acquire mastery of a unique combination of technical, analytical, business, and leadership skills as depicted below.

Table 8. Business Analyst Skills

Technical	Analysis	Business	Leadership
Systems engineering concepts and principles	Fundamentals of business analysis	Business process improvement and reengineering	Fundamentals of project management
Complex modeling techniques	Ability to conceptualize and think creatively	Strategic and business planning	Capacity to articulate vision
Communication of technical concepts to nontechnical audiences	Techniques to plan, document, analyze, trace, and manage requirements	Communication of business concepts to technical audiences	Organizational change management, management of power and politics
Testing, verification, and validation	Requirements risk assessment and management	Business outcome thinking	Problem solving, negotiation, and decision making
Technical writing	Administrative, analytical, and reporting skills	Business writing	Team management, leadership, mentoring, and facilitation
Rapid prototyping	Cost/benefit analysis	Business case development	Authenticity, ethics, and integrity
Technical domain knowledge	Time management and personal organization	Business domain knowledge	Customer relationship management

Putting It All Together

So what does this mean for the BA? If you are a practicing BA, determine the complexity of your current project assignments and identify gaps in the capabilities needed to be successful. If you have significant gaps in BA capabilities on your project, work with the PM and your BA practice lead to fill the gaps with experienced BAs as coaches and consultants to your project team. In addition, identify the level of BA work you aspire to, and draft your personal learning and development plan to achieve the level of your choice.

So What Does This Mean for the BA Practice Lead?

This chapter presents a case to help a BA practice lead methodically build a capable BA workforce. Use these tools and this broad approach for BA team recruiting and development to build your world-clas0073ccddxc BA practice.

Reference
Hass, Kathleen B. *Managing Complex Projects: A New Model*.
Vienna, VA: Management Concepts, Inc., 2009.

Kathleen B. (Kitty) Hass, PMP
Senior Practice Consultant
Kathleen Hass & Associates, Inc.
Email: kittyhass@comcast.net
Website: www.kathleenhass.com

Kitty is the president of her consulting practice specializing in enterprise business analysis, complex project management, and strategy execution through portfolio management. She is a prominent presenter at industry conferences, author, and facilitator. In addition to assessments, Kitty's expertise includes implementing and managing PMOs and BACOEs, coaching critical project teams, and managing large complex programs. She has authored numerous white papers and articles on leading-edge business practices, the renowned series entitled *Business Analysis Essential Library,* and the PMI Book of the Year *Managing Project Complexity - A New Model.* Kitty is serving as a Director on the International Institute of Business Analysis (IIBA) Board from 2008 to 2016.

19

What, Not *Who* or *How*—Getting to the Essence

Alec Sharp

The Key Point

A few years ago, I was absent-mindedly scanning my Twitter stream when one tweet grabbed my attention. Stephanie Nicolaou, then a university student studying computer science in the UK, tweeted, "Hmm, I wonder if companies/analysts actually sit there and think, 'Oh, I know, let's go through Brooks' Essential/Accidental difficulties …'" I instantly thought, "Why, *yes,* we do."

One way or another, I use the *essence vs. accident* distinction on most of my consulting engagements. I'm more likely to describe the concept as "separating the *what* from the *who* and the *how*" instead of "essence vs. accident," and some of you will say "logical vs. physical," but the concepts are the same. I copied Stephanie's tweet and filed it away, sure I'd use it someday.

A few years later, that time is here. Stephanie is now a successful business analyst (BA) based in London, and I'm writing this chapter on "my one best piece of advice for business analysts." That, if it isn't obvious by now, is to learn and apply the concept of essence vs. accident.

Stephanie's tweet referred to a landmark 1986 article by Fred Brooks, "No Silver Bullet—Essence and Accidents of Software Engineering." You might recognize Fred Brooks' name from his book *The Mythical Man-Month*, which has been described as "one of the most important works in the history of computer and software design." Brooks took us back to the ancient Greeks and their philosophical concept of "separating the essence from the accident," so it's hardly a new topic. New or not, experienced BAs often forget it, and many new BAs have either never been taught it or haven't had its importance emphasized. That's a shame—the principle has been fundamental to my consulting practice for more than 30 years.

Brooks' article used the standard example, a cup, to illustrate that *essence* refers to the significant part—the properties something must have to be whatever it is. The *essence* of a cup is that it is a handheld container to drink liquids from, and a *cup* has some *essential* properties—you can hold it in your hand, it can hold a liquid, and you can drink from it. Remove any of these properties, and it isn't a cup anymore. The *accidental* properties are ones that don't affect the essence, such as size, shape, color, and material. A paper takeout coffee cup and a bone china teacup are each, essentially, a cup.

Brooks used the concept to illustrate that the accidental aspects of systems development (for example, programming) get easier with each new generation of programming languages and application development environments. Nothing, however, would make determining the essence any easier. Depressing, on one hand, but on the other, that's why business analysis becomes more important all the time.

Essence and Accident in Business Analysis

Applying the idea in business analysis, *essence* refers to the fundamental, necessary aspects of the businesses we study. For instance, in analyzing a business process, the *essence* might include *what* processes are essential (hence, the term *essence*) to the business—develop product, fill order, resolve customer issues, and so on. No matter how the business is organized, or what technology it uses, it must *develop products, fill orders, and resolve customer issues*. *Accident* refers to *implementation* details, which depend completely on the *design* of the processes, procedures, jobs, systems, and so on. One factor is *who* carries out a particular activity—does the sales rep enter the order, a customer service rep, or the customer? Another is *how* it is supported—a paper form, a screen in the CRM system, or a web page?

Interesting—perhaps—but why is this an important concept for BAs? Because, as we'll see, BAs and the businesses they analyze can be so hung up on the current who and how, they lose sight of what must be accomplished, leading to requirements that miss the point and solutions that perpetuate the past. To illustrate, let's go back to when I first learned the concept, several years before "No Silver Bullet" was published.

Learning the Concept

In the late 1970s, at the beginning of my career, I worked as a DBA (database administrator) for a large telecom operator. My days were spent generating control blocks, tuning databases and, on a good day, wading through hexadecimal dumps in search of broken pointers. Life was good. I certainly wasn't a BA, but that was about to change.

My *big break* came when I was assigned to do the database design for the Treasury Department's new system for tracking bonds and shares. This was a critical application because of the need to continuously monitor holdings in the company. The goal, never written down, was to keep one particular investor in check.

Oh, oh...

The project had already been under way for a year (clearly, pre-Agile) when I arranged a meeting with the systems analyst/project manager who'd been running it as a one-man show. I expected a full rundown of the proposed application's functionality and specific requirements. To put it mildly, that was not the case. There was some hand waving and generalities, and not much else. It was a short meeting.

After, I investigated a little and made two unsettling discoveries:
1. He was gathering requirements, not by working with the people in Treasury, but by reading textbooks. US textbooks. In addition, this was a Canadian company!
2. The clients in the Treasury had lost faith in the fellow, and no longer had much contact with him.

In short, there was nothing from which I could develop a database design. At a loss, I explained the situation to the woman who occasionally appeared in the cubicle next to mine. She'd become a sort of mentor, and her advice was terse. "Read this," she said, as she tossed Gane and Sarson's classic *Structured Systems Analysis (SSA)* on my desk.

A Way Forward

Over the next few weeks, I read some SSA in the evening and applied what I'd learned the next day. I orchestrated a few clandestine whiteboard sessions with Treasury staff, who were thrilled that someone from the IS department cared what they did. Following *SSA*'s advice, we developed a set of "current physical" Dataflow Diagrams (DFDs) that everyone felt were an excellent representation of how the

Treasury currently worked. It was my first foray into visual business modeling.

Bonus! When the systems analyst/project manager in charge of the project abruptly resigned, and I pulled out the stack of DFDs I'd developed in guerilla mode, I was the hero of the day. From then on, I was sold on the use of model-driven techniques. Management was also sold, so I didn't have to work undercover anymore; we could apply SSA as it was intended.

The Essence of Structured Systems Analysis

For me, the most important aspect of SSA wasn't the Dataflow Diagramming technique it introduced; it was the progression through three perspectives on the business:

1. *Current physical*—a model (a DFD) of the "as-is" business operation showing not just *what* was done, but also *who and how*
2. *Logical—a model of the essential activities showing only what had to be done*
3. *Future physical—a model of the proposed, "to-be" operation showing who and how would accomplish what had to be done.*

Sometimes, there was such fundamental rethinking of the business that a "current logical" and "future logical" were developed—we were *reengineering* before the term was coined.

Applying the Technique and the Big "Aha!"

The current physical DFDs we had already developed were very clear about *how* things were done, and *who* did the work. They showed trading information transmitted from the Registrar in bulk by a courier, data entry by clerical staff in batches of 25, approval by a Treasury supervisor, submission to the batch system for update, and so on.

Developing those as-is DFDs with Treasury was surprisingly easy because we focused on "who does what, when." There was no effort to abstract from the reality of people's daily work into the unfamiliar territory of "*what* are you actually *doing*?" That's an important principle; it's often easier for the BA and the business to describe the *who* and *how* first, and then pull the *what* out of that.

The Big "Aha!"

Identifying *what* was accomplished—the logical DFD—was a turning point in the project. Once the implementation details—transmission of paper trading ledgers by a courier, the batching, the data entry, and so on—were stripped away, they saw that a

This helped the Treasury see that a move to online operations was the way to go. They were sure that batch operations were safer and more cost-effective until they saw the essence of their business. Then, clearly, they saw that online operations would result in less effort on their part and provide *more* responsive information access. We developed a future physical DFD reflecting this, and in the end, it was a very successful project.

Reinforcing the Lesson

In the early 1990s, I was drawn into business process reengineering (BPR), which is when I learned, with forehead-smacking clarity, how important it was to help organizations see the *what vs. who or how* distinction.

I was flying into the States weekly, consulting at a very large state agency. One responsibility was to improve the process to issue business licenses to retail operations. This required a physical inspection of the business premises by an agency field inspector. That part of the "Issue Business License" process went like this:

1. Field Inspector inspects the business location, noting if each

item on the form has been satisfied.

2. Field Inspector completes several inspections, driving between each, before returning to the field office late in the day.

3. Field Inspector telephones the agency's head office and connects with a Head Office Transcription Clerk.

4. Field Inspector reads each Inspection Report while the Head Office Transcription Clerk transcribes it (surprise!) onto a Head Office Transcription Report (surprise again!).

5. At the end of each day, the Head Office Transcription Clerk sends the Head Office Transcription Reports to Data Entry (in Data Entry, there are three batches a week, but we'll ignore the batches for this example; it's already strange enough .

6. Data Entry enters each batch of Head Office Transcription Reports into the Field Inspection System, and then routes the Head Office Transcription Reports back to the Head Office Transcription Clerk by Internal Mail, who files them by Business ID.

7. The Field Inspection System runs overnight, three times a week, updating the agency's files with the information from the Head Office Transcription Report. The Field Inspection System also prints (in triplicate) all Head Office Inspection Reports in the batch.

8. The triplicate-printed output is separated by the computer operator.

9. The Head Office Inspection Reports are forwarded by Internal Mail to the Head Office Transcription Clerk or someone in that section.

10. Each Head Office Inspection Report is matched to the corresponding Head Office Transcription Report, and the pairs of reports are grouped into batches, one batch per field office.

11. The batches are sent to Mailroom Services, by Internal Mail, and mailed to the field offices.

12. At the field office, the Field Inspector separates each pair of reports (the Head Office Inspection Report and the Head Office Transcription Report) and matches them with the original Inspection Report.

13. The Field Inspector compares all three documents to ensure the original Inspection Report was transcribed and entered correctly.
14. If a discrepancy is found... well, you just don't want to know what happens then. Let's just stop describing this process now.

Even by the standards of the time, this was a truly astonishing process. But wait; it gets better ...

(Here's an exercise for you. Draw a swim-lane diagram for this process, ensuring you include *all* the actors, steps, systems, and so on to accurately represent the *who* and *how* of the process.)

Improvement Opportunities

After mapping the "Conduct Premise Inspection" subprocess, I had the group look for improvement opportunities. If the process was surprising, the ideas that emerged were astonishing. Suggestions included:

1. The Field Inspector could be issued a mobile phone to contact the Head Office Transcription Clerk after every inspection, rather than waiting until the end of the day.
2. The field offices could be equipped with scanners so the Field Inspector could scan the Inspection Reports and e-mail them to the Head Office Transcription Clerk, who would print them and then transcribe them onto Head Office Transcription Reports.
3. The Field Inspection System could be run daily, instead of just three times a week.
4. At the head office, paperwork could be hand-delivered, rather than using Internal Mail. (That was rejected immediately, because it violated the collective agreement—only Internal Mail is allowed to deliver materials in the office.)
5. A courier could be used to deliver the documents back to the field office, instead of relying on the Postal Service.
6. ... and many more, too tragic to enumerate.

Do you see what happened? Agency staff were so fixated on the *who and how* of the current implementation, they'd lost sight of *what* was fundamentally accomplished. All their ideas for improvement were based on the context of "how we do things now," rather than "what do we essentially have to do, and what's the best design for accomplishing it?" That's why you never know the *real* requirements until the context of a future state design has been established, and why requirements that contain no design elements ultimately fail.

I observed gently that, in all this, there was probably only one *essential* activity—Conduct Inspection. Everything else is *accident*—the outcome of a particular paper-based, batch-oriented design. We then stepped back and looked at the entire end-to-end Issue Business License process and identified its essential activities. Accept Application, Schedule Inspection, Conduct Premise Inspection, Confirm Business Status, and so on, which allowed us to design an all-new process with none of the as-is constraints.

A Satisfying Outcome

Later, I helped the agency identify about 25 end-to-end processes (like Issue Business License) that made up its core business and the approximately 130 essential activities they included. I was more than a little pleased when the director told me, "This is the clearest description of our business I've ever seen." Mission accomplished.

Applying the Concept in Other Ways

Of course, there's more to business analysis than business processes. When I conduct a complete, model-driven business analysis and requirements specification, I use the "five-layer" framework I've developed over the years. Here's an overview:

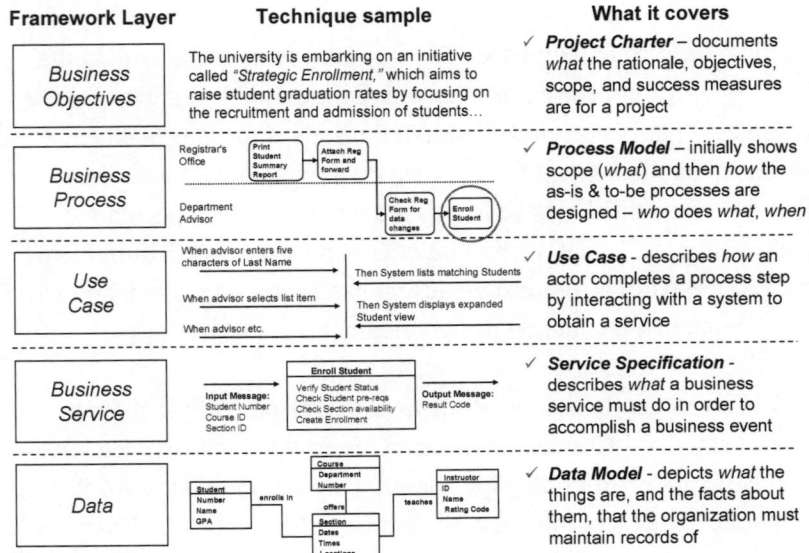

FIGURE 15. Five-layer Framework

On top are your objectives, which are not usually captured in visual models. The modeling happens in the bottom four layers, which can be summarized as "Process—Application—Data." Let's summarize, from top to bottom:

- An enterprise, or an area in an enterprise, establishes *goals and objectives*.
- Achieving these goals and objectives depends in large part on effective business processes.
- At different points in a business process, a person will complete a step by interacting with an information system, and this interaction can be described in a use case.
- The use case is a means for that person to obtain a particular business service (a function) from an information system.
- The business service reads from stored data for validation purposes, and then updates data for recordkeeping purposes.

Remember; this is a simple overview of the framework. Entire books have been written on each of these topics (I should know; my business process book *Workflow Modeling* is more than 400 pages, and

I sweated bullets on each). Here, we'll use the framework to illustrate the different perspectives in which we can apply *what* vs. *who* and *how*.

Business Processes

We demonstrated this with "Issue Business License," so I'll just summarize the approach:

- Identify what business process you will analyze.
- Develop a flow model of the as-is process, incorporating the who and how.
- Abstract from this the essential activities—the what—that comprise the process.
- Develop a to-be process incorporating the future state who and how.
-

It often surprises a business to see how convoluted the *who* and *how* are compared to the essential simplicity of what they need to do.

Application Requirements

You probably noticed that I've done something rather unusual with handling use cases. Typically, use cases become overly complex when they describe both user interaction *and* the underlying rules and logic. Instead, I separate use cases into *use cases* and *business services*. The use case describes the visible behavior of the user interface—*how* a particular actor (the *who*) likes to interact with a system. Think of this as describing the "user interaction" or "user experience"—the *external* behavior and requirements. The service describes *what* the system must do in terms of validation, functionality, and data manipulation— the *internal* requirements.

This has been very successful in practice because it helps us focus on one aspect of application requirements at a time. It has the added benefit that each service is a package of rules and logic which can be accessed by many use cases. For instance, the service Enroll Student can be accessed by the use case Advisor Enrolls Student (using the Student Information System) and by the use case Student Enrolls Student (using the self-service web portal.)

Data

The simple conceptual data model in the example contains four entities: Course, Section, Student, and Instructor. That's the essence of *what* we have to maintain records of, regardless of implementation technology. *How* we combine that data into different reports for different uses (*who*) is nearly infinite. From those four entities, we can produce a Student Transcript, a Section Roster, a Semester Timetable, an Instructor Teaching History, and many more items. As with business processes, it often surprises a business to see its recordkeeping needs depicted as a conceptual data model.

In Closing

In nearly every consulting engagement, I can clarify things for a client by uncovering the essence— the *what*. Just today, I helped a financial services firm see, for the first time, the vast difference between the *essence* of what they were trying to do (Open Account) and the complexity they had imposed on themselves through the accident—the *who and how*—of their existing process.

So, yes, Stephanie, we really do worry about *essence* and *accident*.

Alec Sharp
Clariteq Systems Consulting Ltd.
2478 Nelson Avenue, West Vancouver, BC
 V7V 2R4
M +1 604-418-3352
E-mail: asharp@clariteq.com
Twitter: @alecsharp
LinkedIn: www.linkedin.com/in/alecsharp

Alec Sharp, a senior consultant with Clariteq Systems Consulting, has deep expertise in a rare combination of fields—facilitation, strategy development, business process analysis and redesign, data modeling and, of course, business analysis and requirements specification. His 30 years of hands-on consulting experience, practical approaches, and global reputation in model-driven methods have made him a sought-after resource in locations as diverse as Ireland, Illinois, and India.

He is also a popular conference speaker on the data, process, and business analysis circuits, mixing content and insight with irreverence and humor. Among his many "top-rated of the conference" presentations are "The Lost Art of Conceptual Modeling," "The Human Side of Data Modeling," "Getting Traction for 'Process'— What the Experts Forget," "Mind the Gap!—Integrating Process, Data, and Requirements Modeling," and "Adventures in Reverse-Engineering—What You've Got and Why You Don't Like It." At Enterprise Data World 2010, Alec was awarded DAMA's 2010 Professional Achievement Award. At the Building Business Capability 2012 conference, Alec was the highest-rated speaker.

Alec literally wrote the book on business process modeling. He is the author of *Workflow Modeling: Tools for Process Improvement and Application Development*, 2nd edition. Popular with process improvement professionals, BAs, and consultants, it is consistently a top-selling title on business process modeling, and widely used as an MBA textbook. The completely rewritten second edition was published in 2009. His quarterly column "A Practitioner's Perspective" appears at BPTrends.com.

Alec's popular workshops on Working With Business Processes, Data Modeling (introductory and advanced); Requirements Modeling (with Use Cases and Business Services); and Facilitation and Presentation Skills are conducted at many of the world's best-known organizations. Conducted on five continents in the last year alone, his classes are practical, energetic, and fun, consistently earning "excellent" ratings.

20

Leadership in Business Analysis

Barbara Davis

Can you imagine getting a contract and then discovering the project is in so much trouble that everyone expects it to fail? How about joining that project and discovering a team so fractured they make the contestants on *The Apprentice* look like best friends? Well, that happened to me, but I learned a lot from the project and would really like to share the lessons with you.

A few years ago, I stepped into a project as the business analyst (BA) team lead. During the transition, I worked with the departing team lead and tried to assess the state and stage of the project. To my dismay, before I arrived, they had implemented phase 1A of the solution, and everything broke. That is not an exaggeration. *Everything* broke. The finance team had to begin to manually invoice about 60,000 customers a month until the defects were fixed.

The Anatomy of a Good BA

Although it is difficult to pinpoint one thing that has made me successful as an analyst, I can certainly tell you what makes me unique. I am unique because of one-part experience, one-part education, one-part personality, and one-part opportunity. In combination, these attributes have all contributed to my ability to lead, and this leadership ability has contributed the most to my success.

From my perspective, learning from education and personal experience in conflict resolution, being the eldest daughter of an auto mechanic, and coming from a long line of stubborn, opinionated people have all given me a unique skill set and personality. These influences have all played a role in my becoming highly successful in analysis.

The truth is, I have always considered myself to be a good kind of lazy. Although most people might argue that there is no such thing, I believe there is. You see, in being unwilling to do the same task over and over again to correct small mistakes, I have learned to be efficient. Frankly, in learning to become increasingly more efficient, I have learned that my performance efficiency hinges on both my ability to be assertive and lead others throughout a process.

This is especially important when you consider that a large part of business analysis is working with stakeholders and engaging them to help identify the problems or needs, associated impacts, and vision for the future. Thus, my work sometimes depends heavily on the contribution of others. Essentially, my productivity and efficiency hinge on the motivation, schedules, and workloads of my stakeholders.

Working Smart

In everyday project life, this means I must lead others. In practical terms, this means I do not have multiple one-hour meetings that are both ineffective and unproductive. I am more likely to have a two- to four-hour meeting in which work is accomplished. This way, I waste neither my time nor the time of my already overloaded stakeholders.

Consider this—it takes about 30 minutes for the typical person to gain full mental focus on a task, and about half that time is acclimating to the others in the room. That means one hour into the meeting you only have about 30 meaningful minutes for work, and you lose the other 30 to nonproductive stuff.

Efficiency is defined as completing specific tasks in the least time and using the fewest resources possible. In requirements elicitation, every time an analyst must send additional e-mails or schedules a new meeting to review work, it erodes the efficiency of the process. Every time the analyst must clarify requirements for developers, it erodes it even more.

Taking the Leadership Reigns

Nothing about my *doomed* project situation was efficient. One of the biggest problems was that no one on the BA team knew what had been implemented, what had been tested, what the test coverage requirements were, or even what went wrong (traceability was nonexistent). They spent the next few weeks frantically trying to identify the broken elements and fix them.

After two weeks, I fully took over the leadership of the analysis team. First, I met with all analysts individually to talk about the project and their contribution to it. Next, I met with the leads from the development and testing teams. My next move was to insist on halting the project to conduct a root-cause analysis to fix the nearly 400 defects that had been discovered. It took some doing, as the consensus was for my team to continue fixing one defect at a time while working on requirements for phase 1B. Once I got buy-in from the stakeholders about stopping everything, I conducted the biggest root-cause and gap analyses I have ever done. The results were shocking.

The project was to build a new application to manage a driver penalty program, and then run it in parallel with the old (and broken) application for two years. As it turned out, the information systems department (ISD) had decided to segregate the code of the existing program across four separate servers instead of a single one.

Next, the development team came up with a design for the new application, which would have been great if the design had anything to do with the requirements. Unfortunately, the design was created without any requirements. Both documents were signed-off on the same day by two different teams, each without any knowledge or relationship to the other.

Finally, ISD decided that because some functions were to be the same across both programs, they would duplicate the old code into the new code to reduce the programming effort. But that did not happen. Instead, the development team decided to program the new code into the old application and just enhance it.

BAs in the Front Seat

This story demonstrates that BAs cannot take a backseat when working with stakeholders. They have to lead elicitation and drive requirements forward, while keeping meetings and requests for time from the stakeholders to a minimum. That takes leadership. It also takes leadership to convince stakeholders that four-hour meetings are better than one-hour meetings.

There are many definitions of the term *leadership*. Some include "social influence," "doing the right things,"[3] and "vision," although I am uncertain that any adequately describe leadership as I have experienced it over the years. In my mind, a leader is any person who

---

[3] Peter Drucker, *The Essential Drucker*, (Butterworth-Heinemann, 2001).

sets expectations for himself and others and then creates the environment in which to meet those expectations.

The business and its stakeholders are just contributors. They rely on the project team to analyze the situation, devise the solution, and implement it, which is much the same as taking your car to the mechanic to have it fixed. The mechanic's role is to uncover the problems based on what the owner says, come up with a solution, and then implement and test that solution. The mechanic does not rely on everything you say, because the perspective of the car owner is limited to what s/he sees, hears, feels, and smells while operating the vehicle. It is up to the mechanic to ensure that the right problem is identified, the right solution is defined and implemented, and the car is tested before they give it back.

Again, the analyst must be assertive to accomplish the specified work within the project timeline. However, project teams, stakeholders, and sponsors must also expect that with this assertiveness, there is a level of coaching, especially as the BA gains experience.

On my project, despite having built trust with each team member, each was still reluctant to follow the new process or have his or her work assessed against any metrics. They felt the metrics were a sign of personal failure, and the new process was too different. I had to be assertive with the team and stakeholders. One person even told me I was being "unreasonable." I agreed but said I knew he could do it. As I worked with the team members to deliver their tasks, their confidence and comfort level grew.

In the end, we delivered the requirements only two weeks late. In addition we implemented phase 1B, with two defects related to driver's license numbers.

Coach vs Consultant

There is a difference between a coach and a consultant. A consultant is a person who comes in to fix a specific problem, and the scope of his or her duties is limited to producing those results. On the other hand, a coach is there to guide and help the business get out of its own way to create the needed solution. It is important for the BA to do both—to fix the immediate problem by creating the needed results, and to coach the business when the solution implemented or the process used will not solve the problem or create the needed results.

Far too many analysts rely on the business to "respond to their e-mail requests," and when this does not happen, they lament about not getting responses or the trouble it takes to get people to make time for meetings. Others rely on the business to "let them know about all necessary requirements." Unfortunately, this leads to missed requirements.

The truth is, leadership enables the analyst to be assertive and write well-worded e-mails to encourage more responses and attendance. It also enables the analyst to have discussions with stakeholders to reveal requirements, goals, problems, risks, issues, and challenges. Leadership enables analysts to guide stakeholders through those discussions within the allotted time and achieve the necessary outcomes. As I mentioned earlier, leadership is the ability to set and manage expectations for one's self and others, which includes the ability to lead and guide others through a process to the desired result. Whether over a single meeting or the entire project, leadership is crucial to driving the work.

The first team lead in the project mentioned above demonstrated no ability to lead or direct the workload. She had no idea how to control the flow or assess the KPIs of the group and their efforts. Under her leadership, the company went from a $1.2-million, six-month project to a $5-million failing project over two years.

Had it not been for my leadership ability, this team would not have changed. They would have produced the same results in the next phase. Certainly, no one expected anything different. In the end, I pulled back a change request for $4 million and helped the company save money.

The Collective Wisdom of BAs

Over the years, I have interviewed nearly a thousand business analysts for various reasons. Invariably, I ask two primary questions:
1. How do you gather your requirements?
2. How do you validate your requirements?

The most common responses to these questions are "I go to the user" and "I go back to the user." To this, I ask the follow-up question: "What do you do if the user doesn't know?"

Although this might seem as though it has nothing to do with leadership, it is in fact an indicator of their ability to take charge and lead the stakeholders through requirements to achieve the result. It indicates a dependency on the user to tell them what to do and when to do it.

Consider this—many stakeholders come from all different roles in the company and may have varying levels of education. They could also have differing tenures in the company, with which comes an uncertain degree of business knowledge. To compound this, it could be their first IT project, meaning they have no idea what to expect. As if this wasn't enough, they probably still have that day-job for which they were hired. That takes precedence over the project, because they are paid for this job, and this falls under the "other duties as assigned."

Now, after all that, tell me whether the analyst should depend on the leadership of the business to accomplish requirements. The answer, of course, is no. The analyst must lead the process and tasks under their purview. In the end, the analyst who leads the work is ultimately going to be more successful. They will ask the right questions, uncover the right problems and the far-reaching impacts, derive the right solution, and have the ability to support the business throughout the process.

Barbara Davis
RQX Global Training & Consulting LLC
E-mail: bdavis@rqxglobal.com
Twitter: @rqxglobal
Website: www.rqxglobal.com
LinkedIn: Barbara Davis (barbaradavis2)

Ms. Davis is a proven thought leader and expert in business analysis, project management, and various aspects of information technology management and business. She is a published author, speaker, and champion of technology standards and infrastructure; and developed the world's first university-accredited business analysis diploma program.

Barbara is the author of *Managing Business Analysis Services: A Framework for Sustainable Projects*, *Corporate Strategy Success*, *Mastering Software Project Requirements: A Framework for Successful Planning, Development & Alignment*, and *Going Beyond the Waterfall: Managing Scope Effectively Across the Project Life Cycle*.

21

Just Assumptions, Sound the Alarm!

Haydn Thomas

"All we need is *just* a ..." How many times have you heard those words from your project manager or sponsor? Or, what about, "It's *just* a project to do X and Y." Then there's the classic, "Can you *just* get on with it?"

The word *just* might be only four letters, but it throws up a potential world of pain for business analysts. Sponsors and stakeholders use the word *just* to get someone to do something or avoid doing something themselves. They also use *just* when there is a lack of information, as in "It's *just* that ..."

During my career as a project professional, I have seen many

projects fail because of a lack of information at the start of projects.
We know that BAs *should* be involved in the definition of the project
and apply the *Business Analysis Body of Knowledge (BABOK)*
knowledge area, Enterprise Analysis and Situation Analysis.

Without undertaking this analysis, assumptions are easily made,
and people believe these educated guesses to be true. They are not
facts. They are not rational. Nonetheless, sponsors and project
managers use assumptions during the exciting early stages of the
project, and as we know, they don't document or share them with
others on the project team. More often than not, however, assumptions
are used instead of reliable and dependable information on projects in a
bid to speed up a process. That's where the danger lies for a BA,
stakeholders, and project teams.

The *Just* Alarm

To reduce the risk of *just assumptions* derailing a project and add
value as a BA, I use a trick I call the *Just Alarm*. Whenever I hear the
word *just* uttered in a project meeting, I stop the person talking and ask
her to tell me exactly to what she was referring. Exactly what is she
after? I encourage her to be as specific as possible. I encourage her to
be detailed. If she doesn't give me specifics right away, I keep probing
until she is forthcoming with more detailed information.

Once I have the detail, I'm in a better position to delve even
further to discover what the person is prepared to forgo if we *just* do as
she asks. What ramifications will the actions have on the project's
triple constraints of time, cost, and scope? Will this help her deliver
against the organization's goals and expectations?

The Just Alarm also can be used when you hear other assumption-
fueled words and phrases injected into project discussions. These
include "well, you know," "it's only," "but that's how we do it," and
"don't you understand?" The moment you hear any of these phrases in
your project meetings, ask the person speaking to be more specific.
This often will force him to articulate his thoughts differently.
Depending on his clarity and the specifics he offers, it also could give

you, as the BA, an area for further investigation and analysis.

The fact is, as humans we do not go out of our way to make bad or wrong decisions. Instead, we make decisions based on the information available to us at a particular time. We only know we've made a good or bad decision when we've received additional information. The problem with projects is that BAs require significant information at the start so they can help an organization make the best project decisions possible.

There are some times in a project when using your Just Alarm will be particularly crucial. For example, a sponsor or stakeholder might come to you and ask, "Can you *just* add A and B to the project?" They might think they're simply trying to incorporate an activity into your project so it delivers an extra business benefit. In fact, adding the activity will at best push out your project deliverables. At worst, it will seriously affect your triple constraints of time, cost, and scope. Turning Off the Just Alarm

To mitigate the impact of just assumptions on a project's triple constraints, I do two things. First, I make sure I have spent enough time defining the project scope with the stakeholder or sponsor at the beginning of the project. This involves identifying where we are today, identifying where we want to be, and then determining the activities that will take us from the "as is" to the "to be." By activities, I mean the *what*, not the *how*. These activities form the basis of the deliverables you will put into a work breakdown structure.

Second, when someone says he "just wants ..." I ask him to *just* fill out a change request. By asking him to write down exactly what he wants on an official change request form, he is literally forced to stop and think about what he is asking. Submitting an official change request also makes him think twice before simply issuing an off-the-cuff just directive he hasn't thought through.

From my experience, nearly 90 percent of all written change requests achieve the goal of helping the project team understand the specifics of a directive. Getting into the habit of *just* filling out a change request also will help you document the assumptions as they arise throughout the project life cycle.

Listing Project Assumptions

Another good habit to get into is to list all project assumptions in an assumptions analysis document and include this in your project charter. For this assumptions analysis document, I like to categorize assumptions under the following headings: resource availability, project funding, access to available resources, operational acceptance, level of quality, alignment to strategy, level of competency, security level, access to relevant and timely data, and timeliness of decision making. You can also add categories for "go" and "no-go" decisions, interface alignment, commitment, accuracy, innovation, complexity, and integration.

It's important to note that this process of chunking down the assumptions analysis isn't supposed to add to your workload. It simply will give you an overarching record that you and the project team can refer to in standard project meetings and discussions with your stakeholders and sponsors. By gathering detailed information and documenting the details, you will help yourself and the project team to identify the specifics of the tasks.

A comprehensive assumptions analysis will give you a framework from which to keep an eye on specific events at different points of the project. In addition, it will allow you to easily identify any information that is missing from the project plan, as well as flag less specific information that might come along later in your project.

Once you have all just assumptions documented, then it's up to you as the BA to try to turn each assumption on your list into a defendable fact. Ask rational questions. Probe the content experts associated with your project to find the specific information that will help your sponsors and stakeholders make better decisions.

Mitigating Risk

Any assumptions you can't turn into defendable and rational facts become risks to your project. Events may aspire that could have a positive or negative impact on your project deliverables. Positive risks can improve opportunities to successfully deliver a project, whereas negative risks can seriously affect a project's deliverables. However, it's the negative risks that have the greatest impact on a project, so let's quickly look at how to use the just assumptions techniques to either reduce the likelihood of the risk occurring or mitigate the risk.

One of your key responsibilities as BA is to document the risks throughout the life cycle of your project. To accurately capture these risks, you must document the assumptions that pop up at different stages of the project life cycle. As I've noted, to simplify this documentation process, I like to maintain notes on all assumptions in the project and place them with my risk records. Then, I try to allocate ownership of the assumptions so someone on the project team can be held accountable for a particular one. This person is then tasked with learning the specific information needed to verify the assumption and make more informed decisions. I find that this helps drive a more detailed approach, and it often results in greater team ownership of not only the information gathered, but also the information disseminated.

The other trick is to revisit the assumptions often. If, after several attempts, you still can't turn an assumption into defendable and rational information, you immediately need to identify the assumption as a risk and respond to it accordingly.

Never Assume

Detailed business analysis of any assumptions is an invaluable process throughout a project, but it's crucial at the requirements gathering stage occurring at the start of the project life cycle. Why? Because your stakeholder might have been doing similar work on your project for a long time. He might assume that much of his knowledge is shared by others. It might not be.

As the BA, it's up to you to make sure that you and your project team understand the information the stakeholder offers. Never assume. Encourage your stakeholder to get down to specifics when he's going through the project requirements. Remember, you will be taking these requirements and giving them to the vendors who create the outputs. Unless you provide your vendors with specific and reliable information, it will be very difficult to achieve the desired project results.

It's worth noting that some stakeholders find it difficult to translate the information in their heads into specifics. If this is the case for your stakeholder, ask him to show you what he means in pictures and diagrams on a whiteboard. Get him to walk you through the requirement. Ask him for specifics. If you don't understand something he refers to, it's vital that you get clarification from the stakeholder before the project progresses. Highlight any *just* requests he makes. Identify any underlying assumptions. Then, make sure these assumptions are not flippantly discarded. Don't believe that resources will *just* appear when you need them. Instead, challenge your project team to back up the assumptions with defendable facts.

Through the requirements gathering process, it's also worth using some other gathering techniques, such as observation, surveys, prototypes, and joint requirements sessions with areas of the organization that might have carried out similar projects in the past. By using more than one technique, you are more likely to identify most assumptions that might arise at different points of the project. You are also more likely to gather SMART requirements. The acronym stands for specific, measurable, achievable, realistic, and traceable (back to who raised the requirement). By always making sure your requirements are SMART and verifying your findings with the stakeholders of the project, you will reduce the number of assumptions in your project.

The world's top business analysts never make assumptions.

Instead, they document all assumptions and then turn them into defendable facts. Any assumptions they can't actualize become risks. These are placed in the risk record and managed accordingly.

My hope for the profession of business analysis is that we will be a vital part of the process which creates better quality projects. To do this, your focus should be on quality information gathering, information management, information dissemination, and information delivery. The way you handle just assumptions is integral to your success. By appropriately addressing just assumptions, you will gather more robust requirements. This, in turn, will help you achieve the higher quality results that every organization wants.

So, on your next project, try to spend half an hour with your project team and key stakeholders with the aim of specifically articulating and documenting the key assumptions of your project. Don't allow an undocumented assumption to exist in your project. Never accept the phrase "it's just a ..." Instead, push back with a request for definitive, defensible, and rational information. Seek specifics. Make this is your project mantra.

By getting down to the more specific and measurable, you will quickly increase the quality of the decisions you make and of the project outputs and deliverables. Ultimately, by targeting just assumptions in your business analysis practice, you will help your organization achieve projects on time and on budget. True project success!

What do you plan to *just* do next when it comes to the assumptions that exist in every project?

P.S. Instructions for engaging your Just Alarm:
1. Listen for the word *just*.
2. Place your hands on your head.
3. Wiggle your fingers back and forth.

4. As you wiggle your finger, make a "WOOP, WOOP, WOOP" sound.
5. Then, ask, "Specifically what do you mean by *just* ... ?"
6. Keep probing with various questioning techniques until defendable facts emerge.
7. If all else fails, place the assumption in the Assumptions log and manage it as a risk.

Haydn Thomas
Mindavation
M AUS 0410-629-402 (mobile)
M US 866-888-MIND (6463)
E-mail: hthomas@mindavation.com
Twitter: @Mindavation
Website: http://www.mindavation.com/
Website: http://www.mindavation.com.au/
LinkedIn: au.linkedin.com/in/haydnthomasmindavation/
     Blog: www.mindavation.com/IDBlog
Podcast: "In My Judgment" http://mindavation.com/category/podcasts/

About Mindavation
Mindavation (Mind a va shen) The use of the creative mind to inspire motivation that results in innovation, productivity and growth—mindavate.

Mindavation is a turnkey organizational change provider providing outstanding project, program, portfolio management, and business analysis services through training, consulting, coaching, and resourcing since 1999. Mindavation currently provides services to companies and government agencies throughout North America and the Asia Pacific with offices in the United States and Australia.

Mindavation enhances capabilities of organizations by creating ongoing value through comprehensive and pragmatic project analysis, leadership, organizational change assessment, delivery, and education.

For more information, visit www.mindavation.com.au or www.mindavation.com or follow Haydn in his regular podcast "In My Judgment" http://mindavation.com/category/podcasts/

About Haydn Thomas

Haydn Thomas is possibly the world's most pragmatic project professional. He is passionate about creating positive outcomes through effective and practical approaches to achieve expected (and sometimes unexpected) results.

Haydn has more than 20 years of real-world experience in management, including portfolio, program, project, and change management; business analysis; and business consulting. He has worked extensively in large international and domestic banks, government organizations, and solution providers. In addition, Haydn has worked with start-up organizations in defining and implementing structure, business solutions, leadership, change management, competencies, and efficiencies.

In recent years, Haydn has been following his passion of sharing his experiences through engaging and pragmatic course facilitation, consulting, coaching, capability maturity, and international speaking engagements.

22

Six Improvisation Lessons for Better Business Analysis

Kupe Kupersmith

As a business analysis professional (BA), I realized there are two sets of skills needed to be successful. First are the skills commonly referred to as the hard or technical skills—tools and techniques such as user stories, use cases, workflow diagrams, project management skills, facilitating User Acceptance testing, and the list goes on. Second is the category called soft skills, traits, or characteristics. Attributes that fall under this category are communication skills (verbal and nonverbal), collaboration skills, being a trusting team member, and being open-minded and curious.

I spent the early years of my career learning the hard skills, knowing these tools and techniques were the foundation for being a good BA. Without these skills or the aptitude to learn these skills, I would not have been considered for a role or promotions. However, once I was performing the role, I knew my future success would be achieved through the ability to improve my soft skills and work effectively as a team player.

Team Soft Skills

It is more apparent now than ever that high-performing teams are more successful than those that are not. Most of your work life is being part of a team. When was the last time you sat in your office and worked alone to complete a project from start to finish? Most likely, those times are rare, and you work as part of a team most of the time.

The soft skills and traits of being an effective team member are often viewed as skills with which people are born. People are great communicators, or they are not. I totally disagree. For some, it might come easier than it does for others, but everyone can learn and hone these skills. I honed these skills while training and performing as an improvisational comedian.

Throughout the 1990s, I rarely missed a weekend on stage or practicing two to three nights during the week. What I loved about being an improv comedian was that it made me a more successful BA and team player. In improv, actors take an idea and make it great. The audience provides a topic, and then the actors create a scene and work together to hit a big punchline. We don't take a topic and sit alone, and each try to come up with a punchline. We work together giving each other ideas to play off, and in time, the punchline comes.

The actors build trusting relationships in which they are comfortable taking chances and know the other actors will be there to support them. There are no scripts to guide the actors on how to get from a topic to punchline. In projects, the team concept is very similar. The topic is a business challenge or opportunity. There is no script on how you get from this business challenge or opportunity to a working solution. A team must work together like improv actors to determine the best solution to meet that challenge or need. Although I no longer perform with a troupe, I apply many skills I learned as an improv comedian every day to help me succeed in life and work.

Secrets of Great Improv

Here are six improvisation concepts you can apply to grow in your profession and beyond. By focusing on and practicing these skills, you can be a better team player, collaborator, and communicator and help your team be highly effective.

1. Over prepare, and then go with the flow
   To be spontaneous on stage, my troupe practiced relentlessly so we could relax on stage and let the scenes take shape as we performed. Because there are no scripts in improv, we practiced being comfortable without scripts. The more we practiced, the more comfortable we became with one another. We practiced various situations and scenarios so we were prepared for any situation on stage.

   In business, the more prepared you are for a meeting with stakeholders, the smoother it will go. Make sure you know what you are trying to accomplish with every meeting. Even have a list of questions you need answered. Think about a roadmap that you will follow to meet the goal(s) of the meeting. Then, when you have that meeting, go with the flow. Don't go down your list of questions one by one. Don't follow your roadmap exactly as it is laid out. Have a conversation with your stakeholder. Let your stakeholder speak about the topic you want to learn more about and ask clarifying questions to make sure you touch on all points you wanted to cover.

   By being prepared, you can make it more conversational, which will be make the meeting more comfortable and not feel like an interrogation. You'll get your questions answered and then some. The point is not to follow your plan step by step. The result counts. This preparation is even more important when you facilitate a larger group conversation.

2.   Never deny—keep the conversation moving forward
If there were one and only one rule in improv, I would pick this one. Never say no. In improve, if someone walks into a scene and exclaims, "Wow, I love that you colored your hair yellow," you never say, "It's not yellow." That denial instantly puts the burden back on the other actor to come up with something else. It kills the scene. If you do it enough times, the other actors will not want to *play* with you anymore.

In improv, you have to accept what someone says or does as reality. You need to act this way so you won't kill your relationship. On teams, your team members and customers come to you all the time with changes in scope, changes in plans, and new tasks you were not expecting, or an idea you may consider crazy for the project.

This always happens, so accept it. If you always say, "No, sorry, that was not in scope," or "I can't help you. I was not aware of that task, and it is not in my plans today," or "That idea is crazy; what are you thinking? We don't do it that way here," your stakeholders won't want to play with you anymore.

Instead of denying, go with the statement. For the scope change example, first clarify the need. Sometimes you might find you already had something covered. If not, see where the current request fits in with the priorities of your current plans and scope. You keep the dialogue moving forward, and you will come across as a team player. By not denying, you help the team make an informed decision on how to move forward. By not denying in idea-generating settings, you provide an atmosphere in which people want to keep sharing ideas.

Now, this does not mean you always have to agree with what others say. It means you have to accept what they are saying is real and valuable to them. When I am unsure that I agree with someone's statement, I ask her to help me understand how her point fits into the goal of the project. Having her clarify her idea will help us be more successful.

3.   Always give 100 percent

I can still remember a scene in which I had to come in as a boy from England. One thing I was never good at was accents, but I had to go for it. I could not leave the other actors out there. I squeaked out a few words in an English accent and then fell into my standby Latino accent. I came across so believable because I did it with confidence. We worked into the scene that I was a long lost cousin from South America who came to live with family and never lost my accent. The crowd loved it.

As a business professional, you need to be confident when presenting to an audience, facilitating a requirements workshop, delivering feature presentations, and all other interactions you have with your team and business stakeholders. Confident, not cocky! In whatever you do, give 100 percent. As a leader, you need to earn credibility, so be confident. This does not mean you have to be good at making stuff up. Be open with what you know and don't know. If asked a question and you don't have an answer, don't make something up. Be clear that you don't have an answer, and provide guidance on how you will try to get that answer. You can always look back later to see how you can improve.

4.   Don't anticipate

In improv, you cannot anticipate your lines. You need to listen intently to what the other actors are saying and then develop your lines as you go. The minute you stop listening to come up with a line, you are done. Most likely, your line will not make sense. When you are in conversations with your teammates, you need to actively listen and not anticipate their answers.

Two behaviors that are seen too often in business are clear indicators that active listening is not happening. First, people are always checking their e-mails, texts, or chats during conversations. If you are in a conversation with someone and you look at an e-mail, are you really listening? No. Second is cutting others off before they end their thought. If you cut someone off, you have already formulated a response, or you were just waiting for someone to take a breath so you could get in your point. Either way, listening is not happening when this occurs.

Both situations are trust-reducing moves. Your team members will view you as someone who does not care about their input. They will feel their time is not as valuable to you as the e-mail you are reading. Make sure you focus on the person you are speaking with and listen to his or her entire thought before responding.

5.   Include your audience

Improv is about including your audience. We received suggestions for topics to incorporate in scenes, we often went off stage and continued scenes in the audience, and we even brought some audience members on stage. By including the audience in this manner, we broke the fourth wall, as they say in the biz. So many people love improv theatre because they feel part of the act.

As a team member, you need to break the fourth wall to achieve buy-in and commitment from your team. Good team members are not aloof or cowboys out there on their own. The results of the team are important. Everything you work on plays into the team. Get everyone involved in your planning, and consistently include your team in the analysis effort. This will make everyone feel a part of the effort and take responsibility for its success. As the BA, it is your job to understand and provide the necessary information to your team members so they can be successful. For example, collaborate with your developer and QA analyst to determine what information they'll need and in what format they need it to be successful at designing, building, and testing the solution.

6. Take risks

To grow and learn, you need to try new things. By trying something new, you can step out and shed the fear of failure. Doing new things brings a high percentage of failure. You are taking a risk, with fear of failing as the biggest risk. I became comfortable taking risks by performing improv comedy. Not having a script and not knowing what the audience would provide presented the opportunity to try something new every time.

Taking risks will allow you to grow, and provide with a life of constant learning. With every risk, there is the potential for a mistake. With every mistake, there is a learning opportunity. As long as you are open to learn from your mistakes, taking chances and taking risks will come easy and be fruitful. If everyone on the team is open to take risks and push one another to try new things, innovation will happen. Focusing on trust, open communication, and the results of the team, along with the hard skills, will open up possibilities for you and your team.

I had a great foundation in soft skills because I was an improvisation actor. You can build these skills, too, with practice. Start practicing with your peers and family and gain confidence. These skills can always be improved, so don't get frustrated if you're not perfect. Learn from your mistakes and keep improving!

Kupe, *BACertified^{TM}, CBAP*®
President
T 404-939-KUPE (5873)
E-mail: kupe@b2ttraining.com
Twitter: @Kupe
Website: www.b2ttraining.com

Kupe Kupersmith, President, B2T Training, possesses over 15 years of experience in software systems development. He has served as the lead Business Analyst and Project Manager on projects in the energy, television, sports management, and marketing industries. Additionally, he serves as a mentor for business analysis professionals. Kupe is a Certified Business Analysis Professional (CBAP®).

Kupe is the co-author of *Business Analysis for Dummies* and is a requested speaker. Being a trained improvisational comedian, Kupe is sure to make you laugh while you're learning. For a feel for Kupe's view on business analysis topics check out his blog on BA Times. Kupe is a connector and has a goal in life to meet everyone!

23

Pssst ... Can you keep a secret?

Sandee Vincent

I've been a business analyst for years, and if I had to share one lesson I've learned during this time, it is the importance of keeping your mouth shut, *especially* during times of change. Let's face it, change is not always good. It challenges us, pushes us, tests us, and darn it all, makes us grow too. As BAs, we work mostly on projects, and projects are about change. In this chapter I will share two lessons with you; one about how to gain the confidence of your stakeholders, and the other on helping your stakeholders cope with change.

Lesson 1 – Gaining the Confidence of your Stakeholders

As a BA, we hear things said in jest, in the heat of the moment, in confidence, and even more so in times of change. If you are known to blab secrets, your game is over before it begins. Here are my tips for gaining the confidence of your stakeholders:

1. Who are you? Ensure an email has been sent to the stakeholder list by the sponsor explaining who you are, and why you are on the project. You will often be drafting this email yourself, and the sponsor will in turn send it. Then, know you are about to be Googled. What will people find? Hopefully, only positive things, but at least, nothing embarassing.

2. Book a meeting with the stakeholder. Here it is vitally important to get this right.

-   Book the meeting for a 1-to-1, behind closed doors. Never interview two or more people at the same time. They will not be as candid as you need, as they may be afraid to talk in front of the other person.
-   Book the person for 15 minutes, the room for an hour. People will seldom decline a 15-minute meeting. Your stakeholder can figure out in a few split seconds whether they will trust you or not. If they do, the meeting will last longer than 15 minutes. In addition, because you were smart enough to book the room for an hour, no one will be knocking on the door to get in.
-   Start by sharing something personal about yourself, who you are, how you came to be there, how what they say will not be shared unless they give you permission.
-   Do not record or take detailed notes during the meeting. There is nothing scarier than watching every word you say being written down on paper. People will stop talking to give you time to catch up, or stop talking altogether. It is important to have eye contact in order to gain acceptance. There is plenty of time to write your notes after the meeting.

- Set the context of the meeting—state what information you are seeking, why you are seeking it, and that whatever they tell you *is* in confidence. Be sure to state that, eyeball-to-eyeball.
- Before the meeting ends, tidy up your papers, and do what I call the Colombo affect: "Is there anything you wish to tell me, that you do not want on record?" You will hear an earful, hopefully, at this point. You will have to make your own judgement call about what to do with the information, with permission of course from the speaker.

For example, I was performing a sponsor review meeting after a project was finished. I brought along a colleague with me, let's call him Bob. I had my set of questions to ask, and after they had been answered, I put away my notes, and asked the sponsor if there was anything they wished to tell me that they did NOT want in the report. Oh my! I heard all about the relationship with the project manager. The PM had done a good job on the project, but the sponsor had some concerns of a personal nature with the PM. He then went on in detail about his concerns. Hmm … as a neutral party, and business analysts are neutral, I asked the sponsor if he would like me to pass on that information privately to the PM. He said sure, as long as the PM didn't know where it came from. My colleague, Bob, thought we should tell our boss. Needless to say, I told Bob how inappropriate this was, and never invited Bob along to another meeting.

3. There are times when it pays to mind your own beeswax. There was a time I needed to investigate the processes for a department. This was a department which had implemented new procedures throughout the organization, and they were not well accepted, at all. My role was to hold meetings to try to find out the root cause of the problem. By the way, Fishbone's and the 5 Why's are wonderful for this type of work. For expediency, these meetings were in groups of 8-to-10 people.

I co-facilitated this session with another BA, so one of us
could ask questions using an overhead projector and laptop
while the other scribed. Before we even began, we said that
whatever was stated in this room would remain in this room,
and asked all participants to honor this request. We then began
to type up what was said. As the content appeared on the
screen, the participants had a chance to correct the notes as
they were typed, and they knew we were recording the facts as
they were stated. This saved having to send files around later
for review. The final report, after interviews with over 200
people, carried candid feedback allowing an honest
opportunity for process corrections. The end result after the
Fishbone exercise? Because we were known to keep a secret,
we were able to determine that the root cause was a bottleneck
caused by decision making. The rules for the decision making
were then automated by a few system changes.

Lesson 2 – Helping Your Stakeholders Cope With Change

Sure, being able to keep a secret about who said what about whom is
one thing, but being positive, supportive, *and* neutral when people are
going through change is a skill that BAs must master. Those who
know me have heard me say that the PM sees the forest, the BA sees
the trees. The BA, being the one who interacts directly with the end
users and subject matter experts, is thus *in the trees* and is the only one
on a project team that knows how people *feel* about the project; love it,
hate it, or indifferent. Change, even though anticipated and wanted,
can make the best worker anxious. Where previously you may have
been the expert and extremely competent in your role, you now have to
adapt and learn a new way of doing something, while being afraid of
looking stupid. Fear of failure is more pronounced the longer the
person has been in their role. I have seen this often when a person has
been doing more or less the same job for 25-to-30 years, and now has
to learn something completely new. He/she often feels too old to learn,
but are too young to retire. This person is scared, and if ignored or
unsupported, could poison the outcome. The BA is the one who needs
to raise the flag if more training or support is required. The BA should

also be available during and after implementation to allay and resolve any concerns or issues with the new system.

Let me tell you about Rose, a 57-year-old woman who was in just this situation. Rose was the supervisor for a department that manually counted the widgets in the warehouse. She then entered the specific widget type and model in her database (which she created and no one else had access to), including where the widgets were stored, how many there were, and when it was time to reorder. The downside to this is that only *Rose* knew all this stuff. Staff would walk around the warehouse aimlessly, trying to find their widgets. This caused two issues: one, staff were not allowed in the warehouse without protected equipment (hard hats, steel toed shoes), and two, they often couldn't find their widgets, so took someone else's widgets.

Rose, working with the BA (me), helped to map out the current state, noting the issues and risks, and designed the future state, eliminating these issues and risks. Rose was involved in selecting the software, customizing the fields and reports, and assisting with the migration of the data from her database into the new database. All tests were passed, the new system went live, and then all heck broke loose. The stakeholders, using their web access, could see their inventory levels and had some serious questions about the integrity of the data. Bottom line? Rose, where she was once competent and feeling on top of her game, now felt incompetent and small. Rose *hated* the system. She hated using the new system and all that goes with it.

'But Rose," I asked, "you were involved with this from the beginning, you designed the process, picked the new software, tested it yourself, what's going on?" "But we didn't test with my data. I didn't realize it would be so different! I want the old one back!" she wailed. Well, maybe she didn't wail, but she certainly whined, and loudly. Of course, we didn't spend all that money to NOT move forward. How could I explain that to the sponsor? Sorry Sponsor, Rose is too scared to use the system, so we wasted your money and time.

As a BA, I find the best way to cope and deal with change is to apply

John Kotter's 8 step change model (Kotter 2014). Here is how we did it:

1. Increase Urgency: We justified the need to do the project *now* by citing health and safety concerns due to the use of forklifts, as well as the waste of money spent on replacing lost, misplaced, and stolen merchandise. A business case, SWOT, and risk register were created. *BABoK Ref: Determine the Business Need*

2. Build a Guiding Team: A steering committee was assembled of the facilities manager, finance manager, and marketing manager for guidance in decision making. Monthly update meetings and status reports were created. *BABoK Ref: Conduct Stakeholder Analysis*

3. Get the Vision Right: A business case was created describing the future state, and ensuring it was aligned with the company's strategic vision. This future state context diagram was used in all communications related to the project. *BABoK Ref: Vision Statement*

4. Facilitate Communication for Buy-in: An elevator speech was created to articulate the future state, and communicated by senior management at every opportunity. *BABoK Ref. BA Communication Plan*

5. Enable Action: The AS IS process was reviewed, and modified to the TO BE process by the people who *actually perform* the work. A processing model and RACI were used. *BABoK Ref: Techniques Chapter*

6. Create Short-term Wins: Each milestone was celebrated and accomplishments were acknowledged as they occurred using emails, status reports, meeting minutes, and just a plain old face-to-face thank you. We did not wait until the end to do

lessons learned or tell someone about the great job they did.
BABoK Ref: Techniques Chapter

7. Don't Let Up: Slowly, the change was done. This is akin to
   the frog and hot water story. If you place a frog in a pot of
   boiling water, it will jump out. The change is too drastic.
   However, if you place the frog in a pot of lukewarm water, and
   very slowly, without pause, heat the water to a boiling point,
   the frog will not jump out as it has become *accustomed* to the
   change, a little at a time. By implementing the change slowly,
   a department at a time, we slowly boiled the frog, so to speak.

8. Make it Stick: To make sure it stuck (not the frog, the change),
   celebrations and stories were noted in online blogs, emails, and
   meetings—at every opportunity. The TO BE map became the
   AS IS map, and change was integrated into all touch points.
   This included IT support and Enterprise Architecture Office.
   BABoK Ref. Process Modeling, Organizational Process Assets

So what is the lesson here? Be patient, but continue to move
forward. Ensure all stakeholders are aware of the urgency to act now,
and that senior management is communicating about the change in a
positive way. Know that people need to vent, and often it is just
venting. Have a reputation for keeping a secret, embracing change,
and working on personal growth, a little bit at a time. Keep neutral,
and keep smiling, keep your mouth shut, and keep that secret.

Bio: Sandee Vincent is a Principal Consultant with StringBean
Consulting Inc., and has worked as a business analyst for over 30
years, in a number of profit and non-profit companies. She currently
teaches business analysis and project management at several Ontario
Colleges. She holds a Bachelor of Commerce from Ryerson, a Masters
of Education from Athabasca, and is working on her Ph.D. in
Educational Diversity. When not in the classroom, you will find her
on Lake Ontario sailing on windy days, or kayaking on calm days.

Sandee Vincent
StringBean Consulting Inc.
T 416 578 0005
email: sandeeforsail@gmail.com
Twitter: @sandeevincent
Linkedin: sandee- vincent

References
Kotter, J. 2014. *The 8-Step Process for Leading Change.* June 26.
    http://www.kotterinternational.com/our-
    principles/changesteps.

24

Find Your Gaps

David Barrett

In Search of Business Partners

I have often heard people talk about the perfect Business Analyst.
Depending on what association or what organization you are talking to,
the skill sets required will vary and thus the definition of the perfect
BA will vary. But the truth is that no one is perfect. No one is ever the
perfect fit. And more to the point, none of us in the BA community
have it all. So *this* mentor will always advise both the junior and most
seasoned BA to find and admit to your shortcomings. Identify your
weaknesses. And get some help.

Throughout my career running events, launching education
programs, running small businesses and more, the biggest lesson I
have learned is that you cannot do it on your own. That partnership,
co-operative, advisory board; or even one advisor, a mentor, a coach…

anything is better than just you! And certainly more enjoyable.

Call it the power of two. Call it the power of many. Recite the famous poem "No Man is an Island' (change the word "Man" to "person"). They all mean the same thing. As a business analyst, we need people on our side—at the front end of our projects, during the project, and at the end. We need support and we need advice. We need someone or many people to keep us in line and help us along the way.

No Man is an Island

In 1985, I left a very comfortable job at a bank and went out to develop custom software and sell computers to small businesses. A great idea back then and I was sure I could do it alone, but instead and very luckily I found Bob Icely, my future partner. He came with experience, contacts, and very importantly back then—dealership connections. Most importantly, he was someone with whom I could share the experience. And that was important because it was not a great experience, but rather very scary, very stressful and not very successful. I would not have lasted as long as I did without my partner. My gaps back then: experience, guts, and access to vendors and suppliers whom I needed right up front. I identified my gaps and filled them immediately.

One day I had an idea to create a training program for project managers that would be very different from anything of its kind in Canada. I had the vision, time, and ability to do it and I could make it work. But very early on I realized that none of that was true. So I got help. First off, I took a course on creating a new business. It took a year and I was able to apply everything I learned to this new dream as I went through the program. A huge gap in my abilities was successfully filled by a training program.

Then it was time to execute. My gap now? I needed someone or something a lot bigger than me to make this happen. I could not do it alone. So I sought out a partner and found a major Canadian university to work with me—adding potential exposure, expertise and resources.

The Masters Certificate in Project Management (and later the Masters Certificate in Business Analysis) at the Schulich Executive Education Centre, York University was born.

A business partner, a transaction partner, or a partner of any sort will provide many parts of the puzzle that will be missing if you try to go it alone. Most of us cannot do it all. One hesitation is that we are typically giving up half the profits!! But the truth is half of X is often a lot better than all of Y or better than half of nothing. Most often, if you look back, you will realize that the partnership was able to take the company, idea, or business further than you could have on your own. As professionals, in any business, we need to stop trying to be everything to everyone. We need to embrace the power of the team.

When I talk to leadership groups these days I frequently mention the idea of a team charter. Not a project charter but a team charter. Very different. This is the tool we should all use to discover our TEAM weaknesses and plan to fill the gaps. As a team we should embrace the concept that we can't do it on our own. We all have different roles to play but at the same time, we can all help each other. The team charter addresses individual strengths and weaknesses and provides a forum to discuss how we are going to work together as a team in all areas.

Filling the Gaps

So how do we fill these gaps? Let me begin by telling you how you won't fill the gaps. You don't go to a senior leader or senior BA in your organization and ask them to mentor you. First of all, they won't do it. Too much time, too broad a mandate. And more importantly you have not done your homework.

What you want to do is identify these gaps we have been talking about. List them, prioritize them, and start at the top. Take the first gap in your bag of tricks and look around at the options to fill it. It might be a course at a local university or college. Maybe it's an online program you can pick up in the evening. Or a friend whom you know who is really good in this area. Or maybe, just maybe, it is a co-worker or other professional whom you can approach for help.

A case in point. I recently moved my presentation tool from PowerPoint to Prezi. A very cool product but a very different way of thinking. I had a deadline for the first outing using the new approach. I needed help. I looked around at courses: classroom and online, and none fit the bill. So I found a coach. Half my age, but fluent in Prezi talk. I asked him if he would help me. I laid out my expectations and terms of reimbursement (You can't ask total strangers for help without compensating them somehow). In this case we agreed to a one-hour online meeting each week for 4 weeks. After 7 pm only. It worked for him and for me. I paid him a flat fee and a gift card to his favorite restaurant in the end. This is how you fill a gap.

If you go for a big commitment with no compensation, it won't happen. If you go for a big commitment from one person, it won't work. Don't ask to be coached on being a better BA. Ask to be coached on dealing with senior stakeholders or dealing with flakey requirements. Keep it very narrow.

Sometimes you will find a resource internally who would love to help you out—so long as the expectations and time commitments are clear. The truth is that most people whom you would ask to do this would be honored and thrilled. If they are senior enough they probably would have a vested interest in your success and that of your project.

Your *ask* must be framed properly. It must be a structured relationship with a full commitment from both parties. It must guarantee accountability—especially in your role. The accountability issue is a big one to me. I often get asked for advice, especially from young people, on careers, work issues, and more. I typically start these meetings with a promise of accountability. If *we* decide that a course of action is a good one, he/she is accountable to me to get it done, or follow-up as to why it was not the chosen course of action. Sounds funny but I just don't like wasting my time giving advice and not hearing back.

So find a senior resource, frame the request well so that is understandable and expectations are clear. Make the commitment and go for it. The meetings do not need to be half-day affairs. They should be an hour at most. Like any good meeting, it must start on time and end on time. If you need more time, make the next meeting longer. You are both too busy to wing it.

More and more these days I hear of people hiring LIFE coaches. It is not a new idea but one that seems to be catching on fast. Not cheap but very valuable. A LIFE coach will help you through any aspect of your life—typically professional, but the consultation can certainly touch on your personal life and other aspects. Life isn't easy and in truth, if you have particular goals in mind you could use a coach. Many of us could use this sort of coach. It is easier than going at it alone.

So my lesson learned and advice to any professional is to find your gaps and get some help to fill them.

David Barrett
E-mail:
dbarrett@solutionsnetwork.com
Twitter: @dbarrett1
Website: www.DavidBarrett.ca
Linkedin: David Barrett

David has spent the past 18 years building a series of companies dedicated to the business of Project Management and Business Analysis, including: running conferences in Canada, the US, Australia, and India

- running education programs at 10 universities across Canada
- operating one of the world's largest online portals for project managers (ProjectTimes.com) and another for business analysts (BATimes.com)

He is currently the National Program Director for the BA and PM Centre of Excellence at the Schulich School of Business at York University in Toronto and a professional speaker specializing in project and execution leadership.

David is a co-author of *The Power of the Plan*, released January 2013, and a co-publisher of *The Keys to Our Success*, 2013.

David and his wife Karen run an online travel business called SharingTravelIdeas.com. He has four children and two grandchildren; and is a skier, woodworker, beginner golfer, beginner bridge player and road biker.

David Barrett

Passion

"Great dancers are not great because of their technique; they are great because of their passion." - Martha Graham

25

Love What You Do, or Don't Do it!

Yaaqub Mohamed

"Nothing great in the world has ever been accomplished without passion."

—Georg Wilhelm Friedrich Hegel

If You Don't Like It, Don't Do It. If You Were Not Made for It, Don't Do It, Either

Passion is probably the most important ingredient for being a great business analyst (BA). You need to love every aspect of being a business analysis practitioner. The ensuing emotional energy driven by passion is what makes BAs move forward despite obstacles, deliver despite impediments, and show up at work despite having demanding bosses.

At this point, you might be wondering, "Isn't this true for any profession?" It is. While walking you through this chapter, I want to strengthen your passion dimension in the context of being a BA. I want to focus on *why BAs love being BAs*. I will also draw on my reasons for this devotion. Additionally, I want to illustrate how the power of having the right talent can be highly conducive to performing the role of a BA.

The Breed of Passionate Business Analysts (BAs)

Passionate BAs can immediately explain the specifics of their job that make them love it. They get enthused and charged while talking about it and always look forward to taking their passion at work to the next level. They consider their jobs a source of great enjoyment, interest, and an ongoing pursuit of positive engagement and contribution.

If you were wondering, I am not going to attempt to paint a rosy picture of being a BA. There are accompanying frustrations with being a BA, as with any other profession. However, passionate BAs have a way of going beyond these frustrations. As you will read later in this chapter, their viewpoints and perspectives lead them to focus on the positives of this role. Their passion and strengths help them overcome the challenges that come with being a BA.

Why BAs Love Being BAs

When I created the structure for doing BA Interview podcasts on TheBACoach.com, one of the first few questions to each BA I interviewed was, "Why do you like being a BA?" because I wanted to elicit the essence of what made them choose this profession. Was it a conscious choice? Was it something they decided to do because it had better growth opportunities for jobs and a higher salary? Alternatively, was it just an accident?

The responses were inspiring, and each interviewee had an array of reasons for becoming a BA that were unique to each. Holistically, they all had one underlying theme, which together created a beautiful symphony of passion and a strong business case for being a BA. I want to quote and elaborate on a few of these responses below.

Adrian Reed from Portsmouth, UK, likes being a BA because

"I enjoy the variety— no two days are the same, and I like having the opportunity to make a positive change to the organization I work for."

Variety and versatility are two exciting facets of being a BA. The tasks associated with performing different phases of analysis offer variety. You could be talking to a business partner at 10:00 a.m., having a status meeting with testers and listening to their pain points at 11:00 a.m., and engaging in creating a process flow in the afternoon with your team in a JAD session. Often, there is no room for boredom. And while you enjoy the variety, contributing positively to an organization you work for is something you won't regret.

Doug Goldberg from Dallas, Texas, USA, likes it because

"I enjoy the challenge and interaction of working with people and personalities to resolve problems and deliver solution options."

Working with myriad personality types under different situations is a very common experience of a BA. You get to work with very analytical stakeholders and cater to their style of being very systematic, well organized, and deliberate. You work with *drivers*, folks who are very practical and results-oriented. You work with friendly people who hate dealing with impersonal details and facts. You work with outgoing, enthusiastic, and expressive personalities. A BA gets to work with all these personalities under varying stress levels when their personality takes a slightly different shape.

Margaret Marco from Toronto, Canada, likes it because

> *"Being a BA is like being a detective—one has to work to find out what is really going on, produce a vision that others can understand and agree to, and provide clear details so that it can actually be implemented."*

Problem solving and navigating a confusing ecosystem of a project is often an essential component of being a BA. Where there is chaos and scattered information, a BA needs to collate the relevant pieces and create alignment to facilitate agreement to move things further along.

Jayesh Jain from Auckland, New Zealand, likes it because

> *"There are three aspects of the job I like the most: people, challenges, and problem solving. I love interacting with people. Being a BA I get to do that a lot. No two days are the same and no two projects are the same; there is always a variety in what I do. As passionate as I am about learning and being able to correctly apply the skills and tasks that make business analysis effective, I am a lot more passionate about the impact good business analysis has on businesses."*

Often, it's the combination of these realms that appeals to BAs. Dealing with people is not always easy if you don't have the tolerance and knack for it. Working on challenges is not always easy if you don't have the experience to handle them systematically. Getting to solve problems at work that are people-related, process-related, or related to business analysis is something BAs love to deal with using different BA tools and techniques. The best part is that there is no prescribed way to solve a problem; being a BA could almost be called an art form.

The four responses I've shared with you are just a sample of the many responses I have heard while interviewing BAs throughout the world. This should provide you with a good sense of the reasons BAs are passionate about their profession. Each of these interview podcasts are published on the blog, and you can also find them on

TheBACoach.com

A Craving and Desire

Along with all the great reasons I elicited from BAs for loving their job, each BA also has an intrinsic craving and desire for the following:
- Intellectual stimulation
- Social interactions
- Recognition of work
- Connecting the dots, decoding people, and solving puzzles
- Solving the pain points for people and organizations
- Being exposed to solving a wide variety of problems

When Talent Fuels Passion

I recently read an inspiring book titled *Strength Finder 2.0* by Tim Rath that opened my eyes and resonated with my ideas and aspirations. It brought to light a topic so basic and essential, yet missed by most people while pursuing their career. That ideal is that it is important to have an opportunity to do what you do best *every day*. It's the notion of fueling your passion for work with what you are naturally good at doing. At first, it might seem cliché and sound like an oversimplified philosophy of loving what you do, but it transcends that.

The book talks about how society's primary focus on people's weaknesses rather than their strengths is causing a deep internal decay in their chosen professions and the edifices of corporate culture. This attitude is having a growing impact on how fulfilled people feel about their jobs and, largely, about life. If people choose a profession based on their natural flair, they are more likely to be emotionally engaged, as well as competent, which is a given.

Without emotional engagement, employees lack the energy and talent-fueled passion that causes great things to happen when there is room for it. Without this ingredient, the spark for innovation and enthusiasm is difficult to ignite. This also affects people's lives in the end and their attitude towards how they feel about their quality of life in general.

They Were Made for This

A great BA has a natural flair for being adept at being a BA, which means that great BAs have discovered the talent that helps them do their job with greater ease. Some key strengths needed to be a BA include people skills, problem solving skills, systems thinking, public speaking, organizational skills, conceptual ability, quick learning, communication skills, and leadership skills. Although these skills are essential in other roles, the form and shape of use can vary greatly for a BA role.

Some BAs are naturally good at these skills, although the level of skill may vary for each BA. Great BAs are usually aware of their strengths and limitations and constantly strive to take these skills to the next level. Often, just knowing BA tools, techniques, and templates is not enough. Having an adequate level of each of the aforementioned skills is crucial to take your career and craft to the next level and enable you to apply your knowledge of tools and techniques effectively and efficiently.

How I Discovered the Passion and Talent

Throughout my career, I have experienced a series of epiphanies that have contributed collectively to my loving the role of BA. The one below was probably the starting point for this growing passion.

I vividly recall the day during a C++ lab when I had created a program to generate a pop-up menu for a text editor we were building. After nearly a week of studying various functions and figuring out the logic, I was all set to try it. It was about 3 a.m., and I had just discovered how to change the hover color for the first menu-item, File → New. The computer science lab was dark and quiet, with all monitors on Windows screensaver, except mine. Pressing that F9 key to launch the program for the first time was undoubtedly the starting point for me to embark on a serious journey in software engineering. The rush I got from seeing the fruits of my knowledge take shape was extraordinary. It aroused in me a curiosity to build and create software that began as a vision.

At that point in my life, I saw how small pieces of code, put together, could make big changes in the way a program works and change the way people respond to it. By this time, I knew that pursuing my Bachelor's degree in Computer Science was an apt choice.

Participating in the world of software development for the past decade, I have realized that the definition of a solution is the most crucial component for building it effectively. I have played the role of systems analyst, was part of the world's largest C++ project, did validation and testing as a QA analyst, worked as a team lead, and managed an offshore team of 40. Gradually, I started to lean towards requirements definition and wound up as a business systems analyst, which I have been doing for a long time.

I loved learning new subject matters, and I was decent at it, which made me get excited about new projects. I loved dealing with people all through my career and solving problems, organizing, and creating all business analysis artifacts. As a former dramatic actor in school, I brought good public speaking skills to my work. I could map my strengths and use them in the many different job aspects of being a BA.

The Essence of My Message

The purpose of my message to you is to help you discover (or rediscover) your enthusiasm for business analysis and challenge you to use your strengths every day at work. If you enjoy bringing about a positive change to the organization you work for, while surpassing all the hurdles and impediments, then you are in the right place, doing the right thing, and well on your way from being a *Good BA to a Great BA.*

Your Passion Discovery To-Do List

1. Think about when you were the happiest in your job. What were you doing? List activities that made you feel that way.

_____

_____

_____

_____

_____

2. Spend some time listing your key strengths (people skills, writing, puzzle solving, organizing, and so on) and evaluate which are key to being a great BA. Identify, also, which you need to improve.

_____

_____

_____

_____

_____

3. Mentally walk through your typical workday, and evaluate if you get the opportunity to use your key strengths every day at work.

_____

_____

_____

_____

_____

4. Imagine scenarios in which you used your key strengths to solve a problem exceptionally well. How many can you think of?

_____

_____

_____

_____

_____

5. Describe your own story, and identify epiphanies that have helped you recognize your strengths and passions.

_____

_____

_____

_____

_____

_____

Additionally, please visit TheBACoach.com, and choose and listen to BA interviews.

Passion is energy. Feel the power that comes from focusing on what excites you.
—Oprah Winfrey

Yaaqub Mohamed
The BA Coach
T 1-877-784-3222
E-mail: yamo@thebacoach.comWebsite: www.thebacoach.com
Facebook: www.facebook.com/thebacoach
Books:
The Ultimate CBAP-CCBA Study Guide
(http://amzn.com/0988052210)
The Five Pillars of a Great Business Analyst
(www.FreeBAGift.com)

Yaaqub Mohamed (Yamo), CBAP, is the founder and president of TheBACoach. He runs a popular business analysis podcast hosting expert BA professionals, authors, and thought leaders from around the globe.

A passionate and practicing business analysis consultant from Toronto, Canada, Yamo has more than a decade's experience in many business and technical domains. He enjoys working on projects that involve strategy, process improvement, legacy migrations, and new app development. He enjoys mentoring BA professionals, teaching business analysis topics, and prepping BAs for CBAP and CCBA exams. He is the creator of *The Ultimate BABOK Kit* and author of *The Five Pillars of a Great BA*—his gift for every practicing BA.

He is also an executive board member of IIBA Toronto chapter. When not working or teaching, he loves to read, play guitar, blog, podcast, and spend time with his family.

Closing

We hoped you enjoyed these 25 Lessons Learned from seasoned Business Analysts. If you have a *lesson learned* that you would like to share for the next edition, please contact <u>sandeeforsail@gmail.com</u>.

Be yourself, be real, be curious, and we will close with this final, very fitting quote from Albert Einstein:

"The important thing is not to stop questioning. Curiosity has its own reason for existing." — Albert Einstein

Printed in Great Britain
by Amazon.co.uk, Ltd.,
Marston Gate.